FOLK ART QUILTS

A FRESH LOOK

SANDY BONSIB

Martingale
& COMPANY

DEDICATION

First and foremost, to my family:

John, my husband, whose support and encouragement is so consistent and enthusiastic that it surprises even me at times.

Ben, my son, who understands my passion for quilting because he shares it—for computers.

Kate, my daughter, whose help has been invaluable. She has chosen fabrics, arranged buttons, transported quilts, held quilts for photos, and given her opinion "just one more time" many times.

My mother, Joan Brandt, who told me often when I was a child that I could do anything I set my mind to— and she was right.

My grandfather, Louis W. Bonsib, my original folk artist, who painted in his lifetime hundreds of watercolor and oil paintings, many of which won awards, without ever taking a lesson.

Trish Carey, my mentor and friend, who never once became impatient with an insecure beginning quilter who thought everything needed to match.

And, finally, to the customer at In The Beginning Fabrics who told me that my quilts always make her smile.

ACKNOWLEDGMENTS

Thank you to:

The many wonderful teachers who have encouraged me over the years, including Marsha McCloskey, Mary Hickey, Lorraine Torrence, Mary Ellen Hopkins, Carolann Palmer, Sue Linker, Mary Mashuta, and especially Roberta Horton, who shares my love of folk art and who was very encouraging as I traveled and studied while writing this book.

Sharon and Jason Yenter, owners of In The Beginning Fabrics, for having a wonderful quilt shop and for giving me opportunities to teach what I love.

Ursula Reikes and Martingale & Company for believing in me.

Becky Kraus for her amazingly creative machine quilting.

Roger Bogers for allowing me to use his splendid folk art woodcuts.

The Abby Aldrich Rockefeller Folk Art Center, the Museum of American Folk Art, and the Shelburne Museum for generously granting me permission to use photographs of folk art pieces from their collections.

The many friends and students who have supported and encouraged me, including Mikie Tilley, Cynde Mutryn, Robin Strobel, Cathy Sivesind, Barb Galler, Kathy Staley, the Flannel Folks and Button Babes, and especially Lynn Ahlers, who has helped in so many ways, from binding quilts and giving second opinions, even late at night, to grocery shopping for my family so they could eat and I could keep writing.

CREDITS

Technical Editor		Ursula Reikes
Copy Editor		Tina Cook
Design & Production Manager		Cheryl Stevenson
Cover Designer		Trina Stahl
Text Designer		Kay Green
Illustrators		Carolyn Kraft
		Laurel Strand
Illustration Assistant		Robin Strobel
Photographer		Brent Kane

The quotation on page 35 is reprinted with permission of Interweave Press.

Folk Art Quilts: A Fresh Look
© 1998 by Sandy Bonsib
Martingale & Company
20205 144th Avenue NE
Woodinville, WA 98072-8478 USA

Printed in Hong Kong
03 02 01   6 5 4

HB JW ED BS BH

MISSION STATEMENT

We are dedicated to providing quality products and service by working together to inspire creativity and to enrich the lives we touch.

Library of Congress Cataloging-in-Publication Data
Bonsib, Sandy
    Folk art quilts : a fresh look / Sandy Bonsib.
      p. cm.
    Includes bibliographical references.
    ISBN 1-56477-218-7
    1. Patchwork—Patterns. 2. Appliqué—Patterns.
3. Patchwork quilts. I. Title.
TT835.B628 1998
746.46'041—dc21   98-4502
                                      CIP

CONTENTS

Preface

My journey to folk art has been along a winding path. I made my first quilt in the early 1970s. During those years, I made most of my clothes because of budget constraints. Why I ever thought I could make clothes, when the first skirt I made in home economics class in the eighth grade was such a failure, I'll never know. But as a result of the many things I made, I had lots of leftover fabric pieces, and being practical by nature, I wanted to do something with them.

When I decided to make my first quilt, I cut my leftovers into squares. I used everything—cottons, polyester-cottons, denims, corduroys, even eyelet (I did have the presence of mind to back that one with lightweight cotton so the batting wouldn't come through the holes!). I sewed my squares into long strips, then sewed the strips together. After the top was done (queen-size, of course), I bought a king-size sheet and sewed the whole thing on three sides like a pocket. I turned it right side out and painstakingly stuffed it with three layers of batting (yes, three) by crawling inside the big pocket. I then tied the quilt at the corners of every block with wool yarn and slipstitched the open side closed. This quilt was on my bed for many years and I loved it. After the first laundering, there were lumps of batting in some places, none in others. But three layers goes a long way, lumps or not! The nap wore off the corduroy patches, and some fabrics deteriorated over time. I now have it carefully tucked away at the top of my closet.

Slowly, I made other quilts, but was also busy going to graduate school, and then teaching elementary-level special education. When my children were born, however, I decided to stay home with them. By the time my son was three years old and my daughter one, I desperately needed a creative outlet and began taking quilt-making classes. I didn't have much extra time or energy, but rotary cutting had come into being, so I could make a quilt in a reasonable amount of time. I bought only the amount of fabric that a pattern specified, never any extra, and I thought that everything had to match perfectly. And I mean perfectly.

By the time my kids were eight and ten years old, my husband nicely suggested that perhaps I needed to get a job to support my hobby. During a trip to In The Beginning Fabrics, a large, wonderful quilt shop in Seattle, I noticed a help-wanted sign on the counter. I applied for the job and the rest, as they say, is history. I was immersed in the fabric I loved and saw all the newest treasures. Having always been attracted to the warmth and character of folk art quilts, I could finally play with some of the exciting fabrics I saw in them, especially the plaids. Needless to say, I spent most of my paycheck buying fabric, but I was in heaven. Soon I began teaching a basic quiltmaking class.

These last five years have been an interesting and wonderful journey. I've added many more classes, which is the best of both worlds for me, since teaching is my profession and quilting is my passion. I've traveled to the Shelburne Museum, the Abbey Rockefeller Folk Art Center, and the Museum of American Folk Art to study folk art and folk art quilts. And it's been my privilege to meet wonderful teachers, authors, and friends.

My journey has taught me three things about quiltmaking. First, I'll never know everything! Second, I learn something from every quilt I make. Finally, every student I teach and every quilter I talk to has something to teach me.

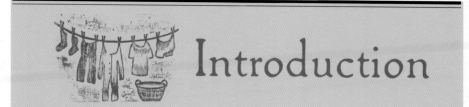

Introduction

Folk art quilts have intrigued me for as long as I can remember. Being the daughter of a perfectionist, their wonderful imperfections have always drawn me in. How could something so flawed be so inviting? Looking at folk art quilts makes me want to curl up in front of a fire—wrapped in a quilt of course—and read a book.

Folk art quilts are less formal than other types of quilts, giving them a warm, homey feeling. Because the folk art style doesn't demand perfection, and even encourages imperfection, these quilts are "do-able" for seasoned quilters as well as beginners.

I wrote this book for a number of reasons. The most important is that I wanted to share the joy and fun of making folk art quilts.

This book will teach you more than how to make a single quilt. It will teach you how to create folk art quilts that are

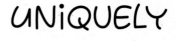

UNIQUELY

YouR

own ♡

Josiah Turner Boot Sign, artist unknown, c. 1810, probably Massachusetts, 18¾" x 44" x 1¾". Oil on white pine. Collection of Abby Aldrich Rockefeller Folk Art Center, Williamsburg, Virginia.

You can find examples of folk art in items as diverse as furniture, tools, toys, clothing, pottery, and textiles. This rich variety makes defining folk art difficult. The World Book Dictionary's definition of folk art as a "simple, unsophisticated form of art" is not specific, but we can narrow it down because many folk art objects have similar characteristics.

Why am I telling you about folk art in general when you're interested in quilts in particular? I learned a valuable lesson a few years ago from Roberta Horton. When you want to learn about something, you study its history. It is from history that you get the rules. For example, Roberta studies American scrap quilts, analyzes how quiltmakers used fabrics, and then teaches students how to create scrap quilts in the American tradition. The fabrics in the quilts show her the quiltmaker's rules for color and value placement. These rules become the characteristics of scrap quilts. Inspired by Roberta, I learned the characteristics of folk art quilts by studying folk art objects.

Rooster, attributed to James Lombard, c. 1890, Bridgton, Maine, 16" x 20¼" x ¾" (including base). Carved polychromed wood. Collection of Shelburne Museum, Shelburne, Vermont, Photograph by Ken Burris.

Historically, folk art objects were made by hand, usually to fill a need. The folk artist's lack of professional training meant these objects often had imperfections, such as missing details or awkward proportions. And because folk artists often lacked access to the best materials, they used what they had.

Many folk art objects look old and worn because, of course, they are. Colors are no longer bright; time has deepened the tones. This patina of age makes antiques look rich and warm.

Folk art, however, is not only about the past. It is also about the present. When cultures cross and intermingle, or as cultures change with time, new folk art styles are created. This is what happened in America. Immigrants brought craft traditions to this country, but they had to use native materials, which were often different from those used in their homelands. Thus, their style changed out of necessity.

Many folk art objects were one of a kind, but as everyday articles, they weren't considered valuable. Pieced quilts were made from scraps of cloth, and once worn out, last year's quilt became next year's filling. Thus, few folk artists identified themselves on their work and consequently remain anonymous.

Certain themes appear repeatedly in folk art. Eagles, flags, Lady Liberty, and other American motifs are favorite subjects. Other themes include nature and the world around us, such as trees, flowers, and the moon and stars. Everyday objects such as boots, hats, and houses are often seen in folk art, as are animals of all kinds.

In recent years there has been a great resurgence of interest in folk art. Perhaps this is because folk art reminds us of hearth and home, of the coziness and warmth that we enjoy there. Perhaps it represents what we perceive as the simpler lifestyle of the past. It certainly has roots in our history. In *Folk Art Style and Design*, Stewart and Sally Walton express it this way: "Folk artists always used and copied particular motifs, styles and colors, and to gain inspiration from them or reproduce them now is simply to acknowledge their value." Perhaps another reason for the resurgence of interest in folk art is that you don't need to be an artist to make it. Folk art is made just as it always has been—by ordinary folks like you and me.

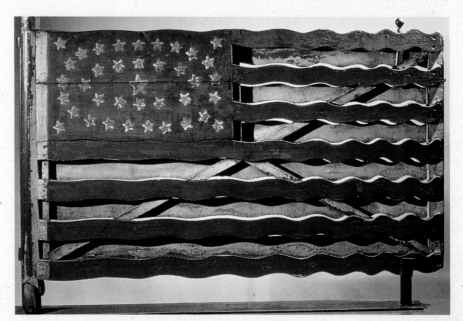

Flag Gate, artist unknown, c. 1897, Jefferson County, New York, 39¼" x 57" x 3¾". Polychromed wood, iron, and brass. Collection of the Museum of American Folk Art, New York.

FOLK ART QUILTS

If you weren't trained as an artist but you've made a quilt, you've made a piece of folk art. You would probably agree, however, that not all your quilts look like folk art quilts.

What is a folk art quilt? Some might describe appliquéd quilts, others pieced quilts, while still others would describe historical quilts in general. While the term "folk art" can be nebulous, folk art quilts have a distinctive look and identifiable characteristics. Once you know those characteristics, you can use them to make a folk art quilt of your own.

Above: Hens Quilt by Pearlie Posey, 1981, Yazoo City, Mississippi, 69" x 71". Hand pieced, appliquéd, hand quilted cotton and synthetics. Collection of the Museum of American Folk Art, New York.

Upper Right: Bird of Paradise Quilt Top, quiltmaker unidentified, 1858–1863, vicinity of Albany, New York, 69⅝" x 84½". Appliquéd cotton, wool, and silk, including velvet on muslin; silk embroidery, including silk chenille thread, ink. Collection of the Museum of American Folk Art, New York.

Lower Right: Sarah Ann Garges Quilt by Sarah Ann Garges, 1853, Doylestown, Pennsylvania, 98" x 96". Hand sewn, pieced and appliquéd cotton, silk, wool and wool embroidery; muslin back. Collection of the Museum of American Folk Art, New York.

Folk art quilts often include:

 Appliqué. Folk art appliqué is simple and often imperfect, as though a child drew the shape. The appliqués can be embellished with blanket stitches.

Imperfections. Mistakes enhance the individuality of a quilt and let you know a real person made it.

Unrealistic proportions. Important things are bigger in folk art quilts. For example, it's appropriate for the duck to be larger than the barn if the duck is what you want to emphasize.

Imaginative color. It's okay if trees are red, purple, or blue instead of green. Colors may also be brighter than in reality.

Floating shapes. Appliquéd shapes might float anywhere on the background.

Asymmetrical arrangements. Lines may be crooked and objects off-center.

Messages. You can use sayings, words, or images to say something in a quilt.

 An antique feel. See "Color Principles" on page 11 for fabrics that will help your new folk art quilt look old.

Mostly medium to dark values. Light values add life and contrast, but these are often ecru or tan rather than bright whites.

Scrappy fabrics. Variety adds interest and prevents overmatching.

Traditional patterns. When pieced blocks are included, the designs are usually traditional.

Embellishments. Although there are many types of embellishments, buttons are used most frequently. See "Embellishments" on pages 31–32.

Large quilting stitches. Folk art quilting is often done with pearl cotton.

Improvised solutions. Borders might be different styles and fabrics, backs and bindings randomly pieced, blocks different sizes, and mistakes patched.

Combine blocks of different sizes.

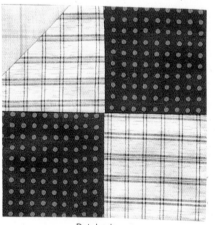

Patched corner

Mismatched stripes and plaids. I cut stripes and plaids off-grain and mismatch the lines on purpose. Mismatched plaids add movement to quilts.

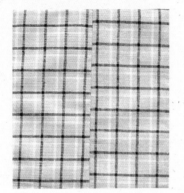

When you use the above characteristics in a quilt, your quilt will look like folk art. You don't need to include every one of these characteristics, but choose at least two or three. In most cases, no single characteristic alone will produce a folk art look. Rather, a combination will get you the look you want. The greater the number of folk art characteristics included in a quilt, the more like folk art a quilt will look.

Folk art is a style. Many different quilt patterns can look like folk art or not, depending on their colors, values, and other characteristics. The pieced blocks in my quilts are simple and traditional; they aren't folk art blocks. When I make a Nine Patch block in two solid colors, it may look Amish. When I use red and green plaids, it looks like folk art.

The essence of folk art is making do with what you have. If you run out of one fabric, substitute another. If you don't have the right color, come close. If you need a shape, draw it—never mind that you're not an artist. Folk art is exciting because nothing is really a mistake and almost anything can work. Remember, in folk art, it's not that you don't know the rules of quiltmaking; it's that you choose to break them.

Color Principles

Start with colors you like. You have to work on and live with your quilts, so you should like them. I've always liked intense, rich colors. I also like bright colors. My quilts made many years ago look like boxes of crayons! I still use the same colors—red, yellow, blue, and green. But now my reds include a range of intensities and values: some bright, some grayed, some so dark they're almost brown. My yellows are often gold, my blues often royal, navy, or grayed. My favorite green is forest green, but I throw a number of greens into my quilts, including yellow-greens, kelly greens, and grayed greens. I haven't changed the colors I like, but I've learned how to work more effectively with them. You can, too.

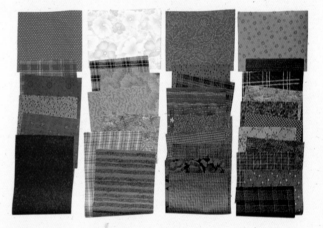

Certain colors are naturals for folk art quilts because they always give an old, antique look. These colors are purple, bubble-gum pink, gold, brown, various shades of tan, and many fabrics with black in them, including prints, stripes, and plaids. These colors are easy places to start when you begin assembling fabrics for your quilt, because you know they'll always give a folk art look.

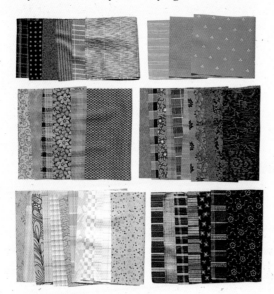

If a fabric looks too bright and new, try overdyeing. You can use tan fabric dye or something as simple as tea. Tea dyeing, besides giving lights an aged look, also darkens and tones down medium and dark fabrics.

You can tea dye uncut fabric, pieced blocks, a whole pieced quilt top, or an entire quilt after it's quilted. I prefer dyeing only certain fabrics so that the tones in the quilt aren't overmatched.

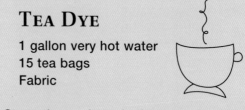

TEA DYE

1 gallon very hot water
15 tea bags
Fabric

Steep the tea bags in the water for 20 minutes. Remove the tea bags. Place the fabric in the tea and soak for 10 to 30 minutes or longer; the longer you soak your fabric, the darker it will be. Remove the fabric and rinse it in cool water. Hang to dry or use your clothes dryer. Remember, wet fabric will look lighter in color when it's dry.

The only colors I exclude from my folk art palette are bright whites (which you can still buy and tea dye) and pastels. I include pure colors (brights), shades (a pure color with black added), and tones (a pure color with gray added). I use all colors—reds, oranges, golds, greens, blues, purples, blacks, and various shades of tan, from muslin beige to dark brown.

Many folk art palettes include predominately grayed or dull colors—the ones that look "muddy." While I use these colors often, I find that putting in just a few brights adds life. "My Favorite Things" on page 36 shows how much impact a few brights can have on a quilt.

It is much more interesting to include smaller amounts of five, ten, or fifteen different reds than only one red; however, don't let the fact that you have only one red keep you from making a folk art quilt. I am only suggesting that more is better. When you use different fabrics that are the same color and value, they will "read" the same from a distance, but up close, the viewer will get a wonderful treat looking at the variety of fabrics you used.

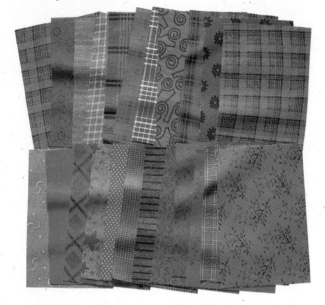

Does this mean I never make a quilt with only two, three, or four fabrics? No. But I do think a scrap quilt is much more exciting than a matched one. More fabrics give your quilt greater visual richness. Making a scrap quilt also frees me from the burden of worrying whether I bought enough of a particular fabric for the whole quilt. If I run out of a particular purple, I can easily substitute one of the same value. Not only does this take the stress out of buying fabrics, but when I don't buy enough, my quilts actually turn out better!

COLOR INSPIRATIONS

Quilters often struggle with putting together pleasing color combinations. I get my color ideas from many sources.

Look at nature. Notice all the shades of green in a forest: the yellow-greens of new leaves in spring, the bright greens of summer, and the dark greens (mixed with other beautiful colors in many parts of our country) of fall. Nature uses all varieties of green. If you like them in nature, you'll like them in your quilts.

Notice the many reds and oranges in a sunset, or the many shades of tan on the beach. Nature's palette is very scrappy! Plants, animals, and mountains all combine variations of the same color. I recently looked at Mount Rainier at dusk and was surprised to note how many shades of blue it was on that particular day.

Another place I look for pleasing color combinations is houses. I see many eye-catching combinations that I would never think of myself. I note the proportions of each color used in the house I like. If it is mostly brick red, with moss green and gray accents, I need to use similar proportions in my quilt.

Sources of attractive color combinations are endless. I notice not only houses and other buildings, but also colorful coffee cups and dishes and interestingly painted busses or cars on the highway. I look in catalogs I receive in the mail for color combinations I like. I keep a small pad with me and jot down—when I have an opportunity—what I see and the proportions of the different colors. Not being an artist by profession, I enjoy observing what other people do with color and adapting it to my quilts. By following a few rules, such as using a variety of shades of each color and making sure that I use some colors that make my quilt look old, I know I will produce a folk art quilt.

This colorful stationery was the inspiration for Mosaic Hearts on page 88.

Value Principles

Value, the lightness or darkness of a color, is more important to the success of a quilt design than color. Your piecework may not show if the fabrics next to each other are the same value. For example, the design of the Courthouse Steps blocks from "Bickley & Bonsib" is apparent due to the contrast between light and dark values. The Courthouse Steps block from "Stars in the Rainbow" doesn't show the design well because the values are similar.

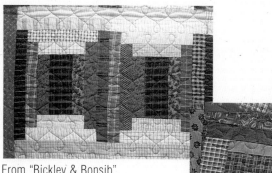

From "Bickley & Bonsib"

From "Stars in the Rainbow"

When judging value, it's important to view fabrics from a distance, from ten feet or more. We see most of our quilts on a wall or bed across a room, not up close.

The easiest way to distinguish value is to blur your vision by squinting your eyes or, if you wear them, taking off your glasses. Light-value fabrics will pop out and darks will be noticeable among the mediums. A fabric with both light and dark values becomes a medium. For example, a plaid with a dark background won't read as a dark if there are light lines on it.

Filtering tools can help you determine the value of a fabric. Red filters, such as the Ruby Beholder, work well because when you look through them, they filter out color and show only value; however, they don't work on fabrics in the red color family. You have to use your eyes or a green filter to decide the values of those. Remember to view fabrics from at least ten feet away. A fabric that looks light up close may not read as the light you expect from a distance.

Medium and dark values predominate in folk art quilts, but light values appear as well. In folk art, lights are not bright whites but are shades of tan or another light, often grayed, color.

I particularly like using gold as a light in my quilts. Although gold contrasts less with mediums and darks than most other lights, it adds warmth and sparkle.

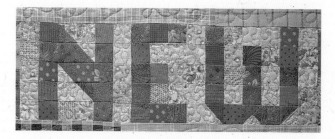

My formula for creating folk art quilts is:
- 50 to 60% or more of mediums, ranging from medium-lights to medium-darks
- 25 to 30% lights, golds, grayed colors, and/or very-darks
- 10 to 15% brights

As you look at the quilts in this book you'll notice many variations of this formula. In some quilts I added many more lights, grayed colors, or brights. Use the formula as a guide only, and play with different proportions. I do.

Now that I've told you how important value is, I will also tell you that I enjoy throwing in value "goofs" to make my quilts more interesting. A star with dark points on a light background may show best, but a quilt will look more exciting if a few stars are light with dark backgrounds and a few are difficult to see because the value of the star fabric is similar to the value of the background. These are the "fade-out" blocks that appear in many antique quilts. Too much of the same thing can be boring, so make your quilts interesting by adding some surprises!

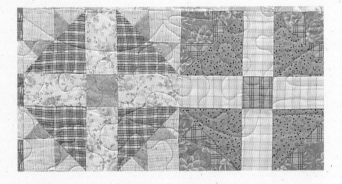

Working Randomly

We all want our quilts to look good, so we tend to worry about which fabrics should be next to each other. Many times we want to use fabric more randomly but don't know how. I suggest grocery bags! Separate the fabrics you've chosen for a project into lights, mediums, and darks, putting each value into a separate grocery bag. When you want to make, for example, a Nine Patch block with fabrics that contrast well, choose one fabric from the light bag and one from the dark. Don't allow yourself to exchange the fabrics. Remember, you've already chosen your fabrics and colors, and you know they coordinate. Random fabric choices work especially well with Lopsided Logs quilts (pages 81 and 84). When I pull fabric strips out of a grocery bag to make blocks for these quilts, I exchange only one of them if they're both the same color, because, side by side, two strips of the same fabric will read as a single too-wide strip.

Design Principles

I adapt many traditional design principles to folk art. Once you're familiar with the rules, feel free to break them. I've found the following guidelines helpful.

If you have just one light or bright area in your quilt, your eye will see nothing else, especially when you view the quilt from a distance. A single light area is like a bull's-eye. Your job as a quilter is to encourage people to look at your whole quilt. The way to make something less apparent in your quilt is to use it more often. This diffuses its effect. I use repetition with bright colors, sprinkling them throughout the quilt so that no single area stands out (see "Color Me Bright" on page 58).

If a fabric is too bright, expose less of it. Sometimes the bright colors I use command too much attention, even when they are used repeatedly throughout a quilt. Rather than discard them, I try exposing less of them. I seldom discard bright fabrics altogether. Sometimes I just need to change how I'm using a particular fabric to get the effect I want.

Put dissimilar fabrics next to each other. This includes fabrics that are different in value, scale, texture, or color. Similarity causes blending.

Uninteresting fabrics make more exciting fabrics show better. Boring fabrics make the patterns and colors in other fabrics show more clearly because they contrast with them.

In general, I put large-scale prints and plaids in large areas in my quilts, and small-scale prints in small areas. Many plaids in particular are large in scale, and large blocks and borders really show them off. Having said this, I admit that I break the rule at least once in every quilt. Cutting up large-scale designs can be interesting. You don't have to see all of a design to know what the design is. A part of a flower still looks like a flower.

Our eyes like balance. When people refer to balance, they usually mean symmetry, meaning one side of a design mirrors the other. Asymmetry also means balanced, but in a different way. A single large element on one side of your quilt can be balanced by several smaller elements on the other side. Visually, your quilt will look balanced, but the sides won't be identical. In folk art, asymmetry is desirable because it looks more informal and is also more visually interesting. Because symmetry is easier to accomplish, I often start with something symmetrical, then move at least one part to create asymmetry.

Repetition ties things together. This includes repetition of lines, shapes, and colors. When you use triangles in your blocks and then repeat them in the border, but perhaps in a different size, you create a relationship (see "Home Is Where You Hang Your Heart" on page 95). In "... But Keep the Old" on page 61, I used repetition by including hearts in three different sizes. Similarly, using many blues in a quilt top and then finishing with a blue border links the different elements for a pleasing look (see "It's Not a Woman's Desire to Be Forgotten" on page 75).

As with any quilt, trust that gut feeling. You can change the rules or even break them. You know more than you think you know. Your eye will tell you when something doesn't look right. When that happens, refer to the characteristics of folk art quilts on pages 9–10 to help you figure out why.

HOW TO PLAN A FOLK ART QUILT

Folk artists usually choose something they know as their subject matter; perhaps a favorite season, animal, hobby, place, or saying. I get my ideas from many sources. Consider things you do and see every day. When our mother duck unexpectedly gave birth to ducklings, this became the subject of my quilt "Miracles Can Happen" (page 78). Take notes as ideas occur to you. If you borrow someone else's idea, change it. Even if you are following a book or commercial pattern, there are many ways you can personalize your quilt. In the pattern directions, look for "Try It Another Way," where you'll find suggestions for changing my designs to make them your own.

Once you have an idea, there are different ways to approach making an original quilt. Some people plan their quilt on paper, drawing it out block by block. Others start by making one block, then another, and letting the quilt evolve. Either way is acceptable. I work the latter way, with a "just do it" philosophy. As I'm working on the first block or two, I'm thinking about the quilt. Once I see my blocks up on my design wall, new ideas often occur to me. Sometimes just seeing those first few blocks on my design wall helps me see what I need to add next. If you prefer to plan your quilt, I suggest that you be open to changes as they occur to you while you're cutting and sewing. However, we all create in different ways. No way is right or wrong.

How do you know how much fabric to buy before you make your quilt, especially if you don't plan it precisely? This is difficult when you're making a scrap quilt. If you know the approximate size you want the quilt to be, a general guideline is that you need one and a half times the finished size in yardage. When I buy fabric, I generally buy half-yard pieces. When I make a scrap quilt, I need small amounts of every fabric I use. I need larger amounts only for the border and the back, and these I can buy later.

Keep in mind that your quilt won't be perfect, just as mine never are, but since imperfections add to folk art quilts, making mistakes will almost always make your quilt better. I use the Galloping Horse Test. If you were on a horse galloping by your quilt, would you see your mistake? If not, leave it. If you don't notice it, other people won't either. Remember, making folk art quilts should be fun.

Appliqué

Although it isn't necessary to include appliqué, many people associate it with folk art. Antique folk art–style quilts often contain appliquéd shapes. These tend to be:

- Common, everyday objects; for example, a boot, a hat, or a house

- Things found in nature; for example, trees, flowers, and the moon and stars

- Americana: eagles, flags, and Lady Liberty

- Animals

The style in which a shape is made is often more important than the shape itself. In folk art, shapes are simple. Although not detailed, folk art shapes aren't cute either. They look imperfect, as though a child drew them. The folk art shape is often just a silhouette, with few details. The focus is on the outline.

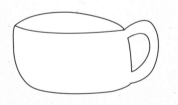

How can you make the shapes you want for your folk art quilt? Most adults don't think they can draw. If you feel this way, try cutting simple shapes from paper. Don't draw them on the paper first. And use plain, unlined paper. If you use paper with lines, you'll find yourself cutting on at least some of the lines. For many of us, scissors are easier to be creative with than a pencil. If your cut shape doesn't look perfect, that's what you want. An imperfect shape looks primitive.

A good source for appliqué shapes are children's coloring books. The pictures tend to be big, with gentle curves and points. Also consider using cookie cutters as templates to trace around.

When you want to make a shape larger or smaller, use a copy machine to enlarge or reduce it. Remember that realistic size isn't important in folk art. Important objects can be larger than they really are.

Be creative with the fabrics you use. In folk art, colors don't always reflect reality—try a red tree or a purple dog. Use plaids on the bias for a great informal look; since the edges are secured, they won't stretch.

BACKGROUND FABRICS

The background behind your appliqué can be a single fabric or a collage of fabrics. You can cut up one fabric and piece it back together randomly. You can join different low-contrast fabrics from the same color family (see "It Is Not a Woman's Desire to Be Forgotten" on page 75). Or you can join low-contrast blocks (see "Quilted Clouds" on page 54). When there is little value contrast, the fabrics will look almost solid from a distance. Remember that even when the background is interesting, it should be less interesting than what you put on it. It's the appliqué that you want to stand out.

TECHNIQUES

Appliqué doesn't have to be a tedious and time-consuming task. If you want to include appliqué shapes in your quilts, there are many methods from which to choose.

My preferred methods—English paper-piecing and needle-turn appliqué—require that you turn under raw edges. Although turning edges takes longer, this is always the most durable way to appliqué. Fusible appliqué isn't as secure, but it is quick and easy. Just fuse a shape to the background and leave the raw edges exposed, or stitch over them.

When arranging appliquéd shapes on your background, be creative. The illustrations below show three placement options for the same duck and feet pieces.

You can float appliqué shapes anywhere on your quilt top. In the illustration below, the chicken has its head down toward the ground. You assume that it's pecking food. You don't have to see the ground or the food; you know what the chicken is doing. Also keep in mind that elements don't need to be centered and lines don't need to be straight.

Sometimes I piece blocks and then appliqué them to a background. I can make blocks look more askew this way. See "Quilted Clouds" (page 54) and "Miracles Can Happen" (page 78).

Folk art quilts also often include appliquéd letters. Apply them using the following methods, or refer to "Letters" on pages 25–26 for additional techniques.

TRADITIONAL APPLIQUE STITCH

1. Thread your needle with thread that matches the appliqué shape. With the knot on the wrong side, bring the needle straight up through the background, seam allowance, paper, and top fabric, catching only 1 or 2 threads of the fabric.

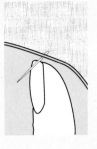

2. Insert the needle straight down through the background fabric only, right next to the shape.

3. For the next stitch, run the needle along the background and come up about ⅛" away, through all the layers, again catching only 1 or 2 threads.

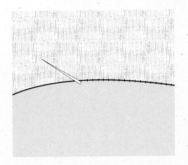

4. After every 3 or 4 stitches, give the thread a gentle tug to set the stitches and make them less visible.
5. Finish stitching the shape, knotting the thread on the back.

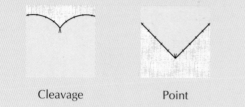
ENGLISH PAPER PIECING

English paper piecing is easy to do, even for beginners.

1. Trace the template onto template plastic and cut out the shape (don't use your good scissors for this). Label the right side of the template.

2. Trace around the plastic template (right side up) on medium-weight paper, such as construction paper. Cut out and mark the right side of the paper shape.

3. Place the paper shape right side down on the wrong side of your fabric, securing with pins. Cut around the paper, approximately ¼" from the edge—no need to measure, just eyeball it.

4. Using a contrasting thread and a Sharp needle, fold the seam allowance over the edge of the paper and baste it in place. You will be basting through three layers: the top fabric, the paper, and the seam allowance. Work from the right side of the fabric and end the stitching on the right side.

5. Press the appliqué shape to get a good crease at the edges.
6. Position the shape on the background fabric and pin in place.
7. Use the traditional appliqué stitch to stitch around the shape, stopping approximately 1½" from your starting point. Remove the basting stitches. Insert tweezers into the opening, grab the paper, and twist it around the tweezers. Gently pull the paper out of the opening. If the paper tears, use the tweezers to get the remaining pieces. If the seam allowance came out as you pulled the paper, simply tuck it back in along the crease. Finish stitching the shape.

NEEDLE-TURN APPLIQUÉ

This method doesn't require basting the seam allowance, but it does take more practice than English paper piecing. I'm not as good at it as I'd like to be, so it's easy for my shapes to look imperfect, which adds to the folk art look.

1. Make a plastic template of the appliqué shape. Using a pencil, trace around the template (right side up) on the right side of the appliqué fabric.

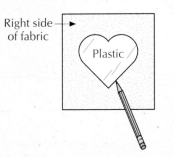

Right side of fabric

Plastic

2. Cut out the shape, adding a scant ¼" seam allowance all around the outline.

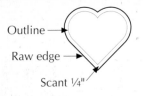

Outline

Raw edge

Scant ¼"

3. Position the shape on the background fabric and pin in place.
4. Starting on a straight edge, use the tip of the needle to turn under about ½" of the seam allowance.
5. Holding the turned seam allowance firmly between your thumb and index finger, stitch the appliqué to the background. I use a back whipstitch with needle-turn appliqué. The stitch is similar to the traditional appliqué stitch, except the needle is inserted into the background fabric just a couple of threads behind where the thread came out of the shape, instead of next to where the thread came out.

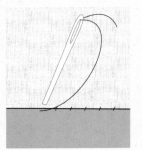

FUSIBLE APPLIQUÉ

Using fusible web is fast and fun. Refer to the manufacturer's directions when applying it; each kind is a little different.

1. Trace or draw your shape on the paper side of the fusible web. Cut out the shape, leaving a generous margin all around the outline.

Note: If the appliqué pattern is directional, you need to make a reverse tracing so the pattern will match the original when pressed in place. Otherwise, you'll get a reversed image. You don't need to make reverse tracings for patterns that are symmetrical.

2. Fuse the shape to the wrong side of your fabric.

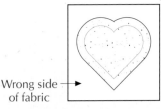

Wrong side of fabric

3. Cut out the shape exactly on the line.

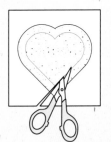

4. Remove the paper, position the shape on the background, and press in place.

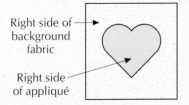

Right side of background fabric

Right side of appliqué

Although heavyweight fusibles allow you to leave appliquéd edges unsecured, even for laundering, they tend to make shapes very stiff. I prefer to use a lightweight paper-backed fusible web such as Aleene's or HeatnBond Lite. To prevent the exposed edges from curling or fraying or both, I secure them with a blanket stitch. Several other stitches can also be used.

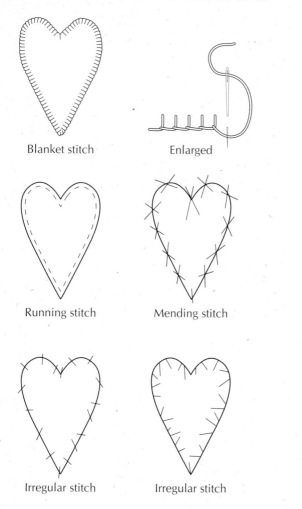

Blanket stitch   Enlarged

Running stitch   Mending stitch

Irregular stitch   Irregular stitch

For stitching, I like to use size 8 pearl cotton and a size 24 Chenille needle. If they are not available at your local quilt shop, both can be purchased at cross-stitch shops. I usually choose contrasting thread so that someone looking at my quilt will realize that I meant these stitches to show. If you prefer to machine stitch, many sewing machines have embellishment stitches you can use.

Pieced Blocks

Traditional blocks help to make folk art quilts look old because the block designs themselves are old, and we're used to seeing them in antique quilts. I use many simple, traditional blocks in my quilts. They generally have few seams, can be rotary cut, and are quick to machine piece. Directions for the traditional blocks used in this book follow.

FOUR PATCH

Join strips and cut segments the same width as a single strip. Join two segments, turning one.

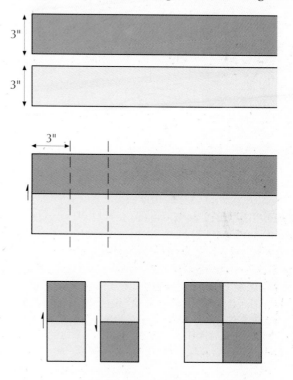

FLYING GEESE

Cut 2 squares and 1 rectangle. Draw a diagonal line on the wrong side of both squares. Place a square on one end of the rectangle. Stitch on the diagonal line. Trim the seam allowances to ¼" and press them toward the triangle. Repeat with the second square at the other end of the rectangle.

NINE PATCH

For scrappy Nine Patch blocks, cut 9 squares for each block—either 5 darks and 4 lights, or 5 lights and 4 darks. Join squares in horizontal rows, then join the rows.

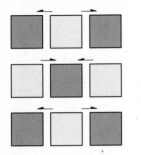
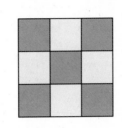

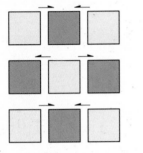
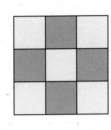

COURTHOUSE STEPS

The Courthouse Steps block is a variation of the traditional Log Cabin block. Cut one center piece for each block you want to make. Cut 12 strips to go around the center piece.

1. Sew 1 strip to the top and 1 strip to the bottom of the center piece, making sure the strips extend past each side. Trim the long ends from the strips as shown.

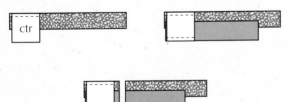

2. Press seam allowances toward the strips; trim.

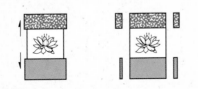

3. Sew 1 strip to each side of the center, making sure the strips extend past each side. Trim the long ends from the strips as shown. Press the seam allowances toward the strips; trim.

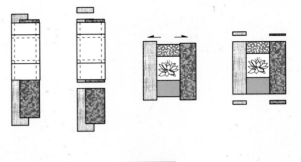

4. Continue adding strips in numerical order until you have 3 strips on each side of the center.

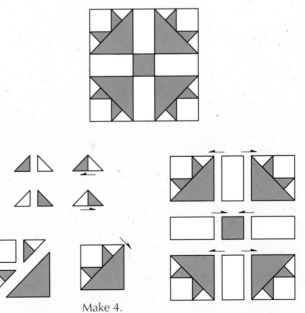

GOOSE TRACKS

Assemble the pieces, following the diagrams shown below.

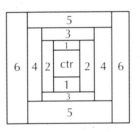
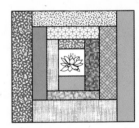

Make 4.

ALBUM PATCH

Assemble the pieces, following the diagrams shown below.

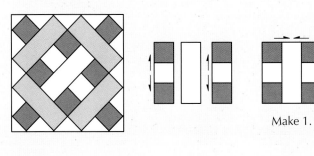

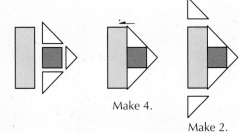

Make 1.

Make 4.

Make 2.

RAIL FENCE

1. Join the desired number of strips, pressing all the seam allowances in one direction. Measure the width of the strip unit.
2. Cut squares from the strip unit, using the unit's width as your cutting measurement.

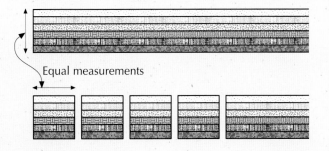

Equal measurements

SQUARE WITHIN A SQUARE

1. Sew a triangle to each side of a square. Press seam allowances toward the triangles; trim.
2. Add 2 more triangles to the remaining sides. Press the seam allowances toward the triangles.

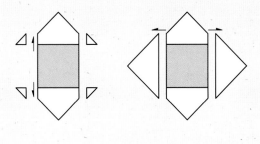

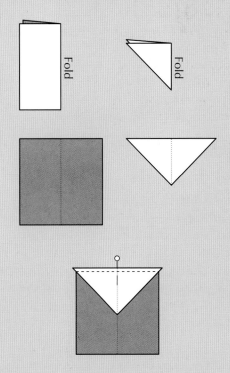

TIP

To find the centers for the squares and triangles, fold each square and triangle in half as shown. Match the creases, pin, and stitch.

Fold

Fold

Although I haven't used the following variations of the Square Within a Square block, I recommend trying them.

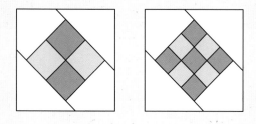

There are many other traditional blocks that can be used in folk art quilts. Try some of your favorites.

HALF-SQUARE TRIANGLES

Method 1—Sew and Flip
Cut 2 squares. Mark a diagonal line on the wrong side of the lighter square. Place the squares right sides together. Stitch on the diagonal line. Press 1 triangle over the seam so the right sides are visible. Trim the seam allowance to ¼", removing the triangles under the stitched unit. Each pair of squares yields 1 half-square triangle unit.

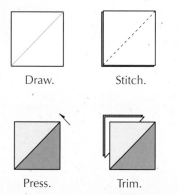

Draw.   Stitch.

Press.   Trim.

Method 2—Two for One
Cut 2 squares. Mark a diagonal line on the wrong side of the lighter square. Place the squares right sides together. Stitch ¼" from the drawn line on both sides. Cut on the drawn line. Press the seam allowances toward the darker fabric. Each pair of squares yields 2 half-square triangle units.

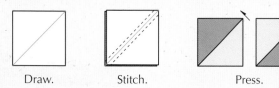

Draw.   Stitch.   Press.

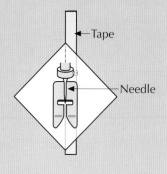

To make sewing half-square triangle units easier, put tape in front of and behind the presser foot (without covering the feed dogs), aligning one edge of the tape with the needle. As you sew, follow the edge of the tape with the corner of the square. This way, you won't have to draw a diagonal line on each pair.

Tape

Needle

Letters

Folk art quilts often convey a message through sayings or words; for example, see "It's Not a Woman's Desire to Be Forgotten" on page 75. There are a number of ways to add lettering to your quilts. My favorite methods are bias-tube appliqué, pearl-cotton embroidery, and piecing.

You can add lettering before or after your top has been quilted. Start and end with a knot either on the back or the front. If your quilt has already been quilted and you don't want to see knots on the back, match the pearl-cotton color to the backing fabric, or sew buttons over the knots to disguise them.

Don't worry about perfection. Remember, imperfections add interest to folk art quilts. Letters look more primitive if they are not "normal." Make them either chubbier or skinnier than regular letters. Make them different sizes and don't place them on a straight line. If you find it difficult to make imperfect letters, try changing hands. I'm left-handed and get very primitive letters using my right! Or you could also ask a child to make letters for you.

Combine uppercase and lowercase letters in the same word or sentence. For example, if you have 3 A's in a word, make each one differently.

aMAndaa

BIAS-TUBE LETTERS

Bias-tube letters are easy to make and fun to play with. Bias bars are usually metal and come in a variety of widths. I use the ½"-wide bar most often.

1. For ½" finished bias tubes, cut bias strips 1⅜" wide. Fold the strips lengthwise, wrong sides together, and sew along the long edge, using a ⅛" seam allowance. Slide the bar into the tube, rotate the seam so it is in the middle of the bar, and press.

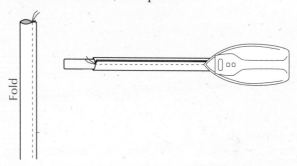

2. Draw the letters on your quilt top with light-colored chalk (it's easy to remove if you don't press hard) and attach the bias tubes with a gluestick, overlapping the ends. I don't turn the ends under, but you can if you don't want the "slightly frayed" look. Let the glue dry.

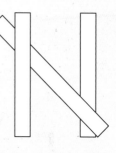

3. With size 8 pearl cotton and a size 24 Chenille needle, sew a running stitch down the center of the bias strip to secure it.

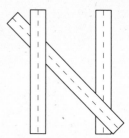

For tight curves, appliqué the edges with regular thread.

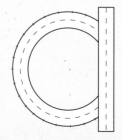

Appliqué curved edges.

EMBROIDERED LETTERS

I write the word(s) that I want to embroider on a piece of paper first so that I can experiment with lettering styles. Do all your sketching before you start stitching, and check your spelling. It's easiest to correct mistakes before you stitch!

When you're happy with your sketch, draw the letters on your quilt top with chalk, pressing lightly. If your saying or words are lengthy, start with the center letter or word in the middle, then work outward.

With size 3 pearl cotton and a size 24 Chenille needle, sew a running stitch over the chalk line, making stitches larger than the spaces between them. This means that there is more pearl cotton on the quilt top, where it will show.

Embroidered letters do not show up as well as bias tube letters when viewed from a distance. A variation of this method is shown on "All Plaids and Stripes" (page 45), where I stitched the outlines of a house, fence, trees, and animals instead of letters.

PIECED LETTERS

The folk art alphabet on pages 102–4 gives you all twenty-six letters. I've included numbers 1 through 9 as well. All the letters and backgrounds, as well as the half-square and quarter-square triangles, are made with 1½" squares. You can cut the squares larger than 1½", but your letters will get bigger very quickly. Increasing the size of the cut squares by ½" to 2" x 2" means your letters will increase from 5" high to 7½" high when finished.

To make half-square triangle units, refer to "Method 1—Sew and Flip" on page 24.

To make quarter-square triangle units, first make a half-square triangle unit (using Method 1—Sew and Flip). Draw a diagonal line on the wrong side of another square. Place the square and half-square triangle unit right sides together, positioning the drawn line at a diagonal to the

seam. Sew on the diagonal line and press the triangle to one side. Trim the seam allowance to ¼".

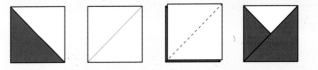

Most letters are five squares high and three squares wide, but there are exceptions. To make words, add a one-square by five-square row between letters and numbers. Or you can use a single piece of fabric, 1½" wide by the height or width of your letter (don't forget to add seam allowances).

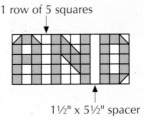

1 row of 5 squares

1½" x 5½" spacer

When combining three-square-wide letters with four-square-wide letters, you can align them flush right or flush left, or you can mix the two. When combining three-square-wide letters with five-square-wide letters, you can center the letters.

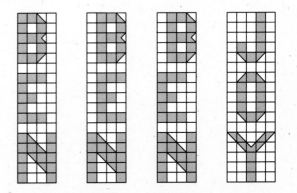

Between words, add a three-square by five-square row. Or cut 3½" x 5½" strips for spacers.

You won't necessarily want to use the same lettering technique every time you include letters in your quilts. Experiment with different techniques and find the ones that work the best for you. Other methods include fusible appliqué with embellishment stitches and traditional appliqué. Although I do not use these methods often, they work well.

Piecing the Quilt Top

Following a creative process means that we sometimes end up with something different from what we had originally planned. Sometimes one of my blocks isn't the same size as the others, but I still want to use it so I don't have to make one more. Sometimes I decide, after I've started, to combine blocks of varying sizes because they help carry out the theme I've chosen (see "… But Keep the Old" on page 61). When I want to combine blocks of different sizes, I follow a simple rule I learned from Roberta Horton: If it's too big, cut it off; if it's too little, add to it!

1. Decide on a pleasing arrangement for your blocks.

2. Starting in any corner, choose 2 blocks that are next to each other. If they aren't the same size, make the small one as big as the larger one. To do this, add some extra strips to one side of the small block until it is a little larger than it needs to be. Trim the excess.

Blocks are different heights. Add strips to the top or bottom of the smaller block.

Trim excess to make blocks the same height.

3. When the 2 blocks are the same size, sew them together.

4. Work in pairs, then join the pairs in sections of 4, using the combining rule: If it's too big, cut it off; if it's too little, add to it!

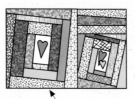 

Add strip(s) to smaller unit.

Trim excess.

5. When you get approximately one-quarter of the top together, work on another quarter (setting the first one aside), then the third quarter, then the fourth. Fit the quarters together in the same manner—add to the small ones and trim.

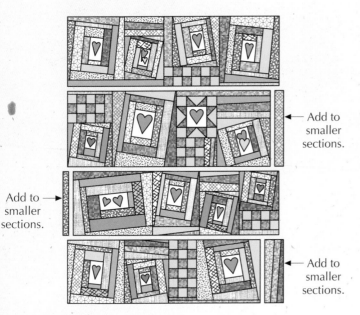

← Add to smaller sections.

Add to smaller sections. →

← Add to smaller sections.

Once you've finished the above steps, you're ready to add borders, if desired.

Although sewing together blocks of different sizes is time-consuming, it adds tremendously to the visual interest of the quilt. Adding fabrics to make blocks the same size also makes the quilt scrappier.

For most of my quilts, I don't plan to use blocks that are different sizes. It just happens. If you look through the quilts in this book, you'll find numerous instances where I added pieces to make things fit. Planned for or not, blocks of different sizes can make a truly exciting and original folk art quilt.

If your blocks are only slightly different in size and you don't want to add to the smaller block or trim from the larger one, you can ease. I do this by pinning together the ends, quarter-points, and centers and gently stretching the smaller piece as I sew. Cotton is a very forgiving fabric, and it allows me to do this easily.

This section includes my standard finishing methods, as well as suggestions especially appropriate for folk art quilts.

BORDERS

For borders with straight-cut corners, first measure the quilt top vertically through the middle. Cut two border strips to match the measurement, then sew them to the sides of the quilt top. Measure the quilt top again horizontally through the middle, including the borders just added. Cut two border strips to match the measurement, then sew them to the top and bottom edges. Press seam allowances toward the borders.

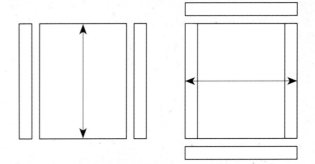

For borders with corner squares, measure the quilt top through the middle, horizontally and vertically. Add border strips to the top and bottom edges first. Sew corner squares to the remaining borders and add these to the sides of the quilt. Press seam allowances toward the borders.

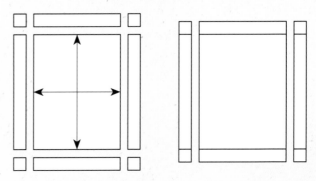

If you need to piece border strips to make them fit your quilt top, join them with a diagonal seam. Trim the seam allowance to ¼". Press seams open.

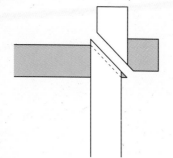

To give your quilt a folk art look, use more than one border fabric. In "Color Me Bright" on page 58, all four borders are different. Besides creating visual interest, using different fabrics for the borders also means you don't need large amounts of any single fabric. I made an even more interesting border, using even smaller amounts of yardage, for "Only One Crow in the Garden" on page 48. I pieced rectangles to form the borders.

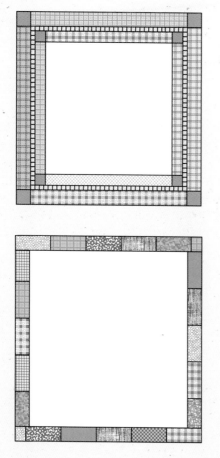

BATTING

I prefer lightweight cotton batting because, after quilting, the quilts are thin and flat, giving an appearance similar to antique quilts. If you don't prewash the cotton batting (and I don't), your quilt will shrink slightly after the first washing, making it look even more like an old quilt. Cotton batting also adds weight to a quilt, which makes it warmer and helps it hang better on a wall. Cut battings at least 4" larger than the length and width of your quilt to allow for any shifting or shrinking during quilting.

BACKING

As with batting, backing needs to measure at least 4" larger than your quilt top.

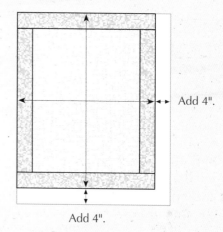

If this measurement is wider than the width of your backing fabric, piece two lengths or two widths of backing fabric together.

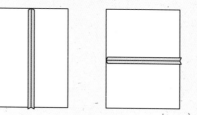

If the backing needs to be only a few inches wider than the quilt top, I often add a strip down the middle. The strip can be a single piece of fabric or it can be pieced from leftovers.

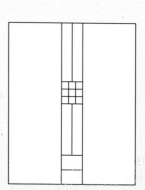

Or, for a scrappy, folk art look, piece the backing from leftover fabrics. Even if your pieced leftovers won't cover the entire back, you won't have to purchase as much fabric. The backs of quilts are important. You see them when quilts are used on a bed and corners are turned over. Don't put a fabric you hate on the back. You'll have to look at it for years.

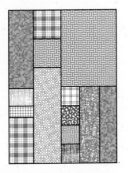

PRIMITIVE QUILTING

Folk art quilts can be hand or machine quilted or both. See "Coffee or Tea?" on page 42 for an example of effective machine quilting. I often combine hand quilting with machine quilting, as in "Bickley & Bonsib" on page 51. Hand quilting with large stitches is one of my favorite folk art techniques. Use size 8 or 12 pearl cotton in a contrasting color to enhance the primitive look.

BINDING

I use continuous double-fold binding that finishes to ⅜" on all my quilts. Straight-grain binding is my first choice because it uses less fabric than bias binding, but bias binding is especially appropriate when you want to show off a plaid or stripe (see "My Favorite Things" on page 36). *Do not trim excess batting and backing before adding the binding.*

1. Cut 2"-wide strips, enough to go around the entire outer edge of your quilt, joining them on the diagonal to reduce bulk.
2. Cut one end at a 45° angle. Don't measure, just eyeball it. Fold about ¼" of the angled edge to the wrong side. Press.

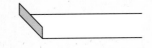

3. Iron the entire strip in half lengthwise, wrong sides together.

4. Start on a straight edge of the quilt, not in a corner. Place the angled end of the binding along the quilt top, aligning the raw edges of the binding with the raw edges of the quilt top. Using a ¼"-wide seam allowance, start stitching about 3" from the angled end. Backstitch to secure.

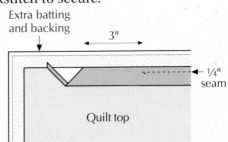

5. When you get close to the corner, insert a pin ¼" from the edge (eyeball it), sew up to the pin, and backstitch.

6. Remove the quilt from the machine. Fold the binding up, away from the quilt, then back down so the fold aligns with the edge you just stitched. Align the raw edges of the binding with the next raw edge of the quilt. Begin stitching at the very edge (not ¼" in, and no need to backstitch). Repeat with the remaining corners.

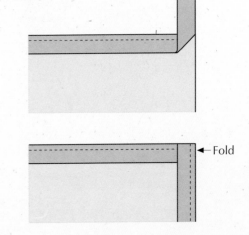

7. When you get close to where you started, insert the binding strip inside the angled end; trim if it is too long. Continue stitching a little past where you began.

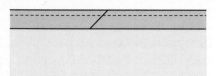

8. Trim the batting and backing even with the edge of the quilt top.

9. Finish the back by hand with a slipstitch, matching the thread to the binding. In the corners, there will be a natural miter on the front. On the back, you make a mitered fold.

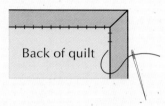

I sometimes piece bindings for folk art quilts, joining 20" strips of different fabrics as I did for "… But Keep the Old" on page 61.

FOLK ART LABELS

Create your own labels from the many templates included in this book. There are also many books available that contain labels to trace. Although I would like every label I make to be embroidered by hand, I don't have the time. For most of my labels, I use a light-value fabric (muslin usually works) and a fine-point permanent marker, size .03 or .05.

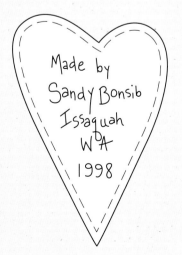

Labels should include at least your name, city and state, and the date. If the quilt is a gift, you can include the name of the recipient, his or her city and state, and the occasion of the gift. Information about the quilt design may be appropriate, especially if the recipient isn't a quilter. If desired, add a brief note about any personal experience that affected your life while you were making the quilt, such as inspirational words, world events, or family happenings. Attach the label to the back of your quilt by fusing or by turning under the seam allowance and stitching it in place.

The most important thing about labels is to just do it. In future years, you'll be glad you did. How many of us have a family quilt with none of the above information? It adds to the quilt's value, both monetarily and sentimentally, to know who made it and when.

Embellishments

It isn't necessary to add embellishments to your quilt, but they contribute to the scrappy look, add dimension, and create interest. There are a great variety of embellishments, but before adding any, consider how the quilt will be used and by whom. Embellishments should never be used on quilts intended for babies or small children. Buttons might look great on a quilt meant for an older child's bed, but you'll probably be repairing them often. A wall hanging can be embellished as much as you like.

Buttons are the embellishments I use most often. They come in a variety of shapes, textures, and colors. You can find especially interesting ones at antique shops. Try grouping some into twos and threes, rather than just placing them singly.

Just because buttons have holes doesn't mean you have to use them. Here are some creative ways to stitch buttons (see "Color Me Bright" on page 58).

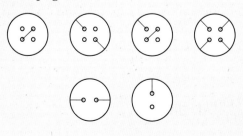

Turn buttons over. You may like the back better than the front. The back is often flatter and shows just the outline of the button, whereas the front may also include raised edges. In "Quilted Clouds" on page 54, it looks like the eight buttons used to make the flowers are four different ones. But they are the backs and fronts of only two different buttons.

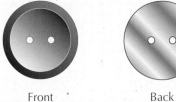

Front   Back

To add buttons, I start by scattering them randomly over the area I want to cover. I used this approach when I put buttons on "Quilted Clouds." Don't place them too closely—yet. You can always increase the density, but if you start by putting many buttons in one section, then you're committed to putting as many in the remaining sections, whether you want to or not.

I add most embellishments after quilting because the thread used to attach them goes through all three quilt layers, making them more secure and easier to repair. But when you add embellishments after quilting, knots are harder to hide. Put knots on the back and cover them with a button. Or put them on the top and leave tails, which is what I did for "My Favorite Things" on page 36. Sometimes you can hide knots between the embellishment and the quilt top. For example, when sewing a button, start and end the knot between the button and the fabric.

Play with embellishments and think creatively. Instead of appliquéing a house, how about making a house out of buttons? Instead of appliquéing bias-tube letters, how about making jute letters?

Of course, there are many embellishment possibilities.

- Consider charms and beads, jute, lace, leather shoelaces, old jewelry, raffia, ribbon, twigs, and yarn.
- You can even use trimmed selvages, as I did for the chicken's nest on "A Duck with Lips and His Friends" on page 66.

QUILT CONSTRUCTION

Prewashing

Because my quilts are scrappy, I would be washing fabrics forever if I prewashed every one, and I would have lost untold yards to fraying. Prewashing is a choice. There are advantages and disadvantages to doing it.

One advantage of prewashing is that if a fabric will bleed, you'll find that out before putting it in a quilt. I can honestly say that I've never had a problem with bleeding in any quilt I've made, but I know quilters who have. Also, since I tend to work with medium- to dark-value fabrics, if one did bleed, I'm not sure I'd notice.

If you don't prewash, your finished quilt might shrink a bit when you launder it, but high-quality cotton fabrics shrink minimally. I don't mind a little shrinkage the first time I wash a quilt. The slight puffiness adds to the aged look.

A disadvantage to prewashing, besides the time spent doing it and the frayed edges, is that fabrics lose their sizing. Sizing is a natural dirt repellent that keeps fabric cleaner longer. It also stiffens fabric, making it easier to work with.

Using a Design Wall

I suggest that you use a design wall when you make a quilt. Pin a Quilt Wall, piece of Pellon Fleece, or Thermolam to a blank wall or large board (quilt battings don't work as well because they stretch). Your quilt blocks will stick to the fleece without pinning, which makes it easy to move them around as you design your top. The biggest advantage of a design wall is that it is vertical, which means everything is the same distance from your eye as you look at your blocks from a distance. When you lay your blocks out on the floor, some blocks are closer to you; some

are farther away. A vertical surface gives you a better perspective, and you can more readily decide if your quilt looks balanced—do you have too many lights, brights, or darks in the same place? Is a particularly eye-catching fabric distributed evenly throughout the quilt?

Previewing Your Quilt

When you make a quilt, preview everything before you sew. Examine your quilt from at least ten feet away, preferably on a design wall. Remember, we usually view quilts from across a room on a bed or a wall, not one foot away (or less) as when we sew them.

 Check the fabrics to see if they read the way you expected. Does your light really look light next to your other fabrics? Pin blocks side by side on your design wall to see if there is enough contrast between the fabrics.

Examine the block arrangement to see if your quilt looks balanced.

Look at the borders to see if the fabric and the planned width work for your quilt.

Check the binding. It may be only ⅜" wide, but it's noticeable and can enhance your design or detract from it.

Play with the embellishments. Stick a pin through the buttonholes and step away. Are the buttons too large for this project? Are there too many of them—or maybe not enough?

Previewing takes a little more time but saves you lots of time if you don't have to rip something out.

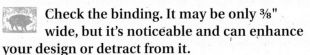

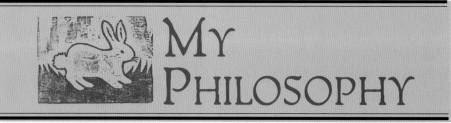

My Philosophy

Making quilts should be fun. Quilters today are not making quilts because they need bedcovers. Most of us want to do something special for ourselves or for our families.

Enjoy the process of making a quilt as much as you expect to enjoy the product. Making a quilt takes time. Expect that. You'll make mistakes. Expect that, too. Not a day goes by that I don't use a seam ripper.

Making a quilt should be a stress reliever, not a stress inducer. That doesn't mean you won't have frustrating moments. We all do.

Quilters are creative. When something doesn't work, we often devise a solution that works better than our original plan. This is especially true of folk art. So-called "mistakes" often add to the warmth and homeyness of folk art quilts, because they make the quilt look like a real person made it.

Support other quilters. You can find something positive about everyone's work. People always accomplish more when they feel good about what they're doing. When you let someone know that you like something they do, it gives them the confidence to do more. Everyone, even internationally known quilting teachers, started from square one.

Learn from others. Try their suggestions and see what works for you. There are many ways to do the same thing. In no endeavor is this truer than in quiltmaking.

Finally, just do it. If you agonize over everything, you'll never get started. You don't know if something works until you try. What's the worst that can happen? You won't like it, or you'll use some extra fabric.

Please yourself. As you make more quilts, you'll learn what you like. Your best quilts will be those that reflect your passions.

THE PATTERNS

Here are a few guidelines to remember as you make your quilts.

Yardage requirements and cutting directions are combined in one chart for each quilt. Although most fabric is labeled 44" to 45" wide, it seldom really is. I work on the premise that I will have at least 40 usable inches, even though sometimes I have more.

Cut strips across the fabric width unless otherwise indicated. "Cut lengthwise" means to cut parallel to the fabric selvages.

The yardage given under "Single Fabric" is the total yardage needed for that part of the quilt if you were to use just one fabric. If you are using multiple fabrics, this total will give you an idea of how much you'll need.

Under the "Scrappy/First Cut" heading you'll find the number of pieces required for each fabric and the size to cut them. Start with this column if you want to use a variety of fabrics.

Sometimes a third column, "Additional Cuts," indicates that you need to make additional cuts to the pieces from the second column. The ◻ symbol means to cut the square (or squares) from the previous column once diagonally. Cut a square twice diagonally when you see this symbol ⊠ .

To make assembling the units easier, pressing-direction arrows are shown when the direction of the seam allowances is important. Arrows are not provided if the pressing direction doesn't matter. In these cases, press the seam allowances the way you prefer. When joining blocks in horizontal rows, press the seam allowances in opposite directions from row to row.

The cut sizes of side and corner triangles are larger than necessary. I prefer to trim a little fabric rather than not have enough.

Cutting dimensions are provided for border strips; however, it's always a good idea to measure your quilt top before adding borders (see page 28).

In many of the quilts, the binding is cut on the bias to show off a stripe or plaid, and yardage is given accordingly. If you prefer straight-grain binding, you won't need as much fabric.

Pearl cotton can be used for both hand and machine quilting. To use size 8 pearl cotton on your machine, use a Schmetz Topstitch Needle (130N), size 100/16. For size 12 pearl cotton, use a standard 80/12 needle.

The quilts in this book are meant to be idea starters. At the end of the directions for each quilt, there is an idea for making the quilt, or parts of it, another way. Don't hesitate to change the quilts to fit your needs. Try mixing and matching your favorite blocks from different quilts. Remember, this should be fun.

> For their hands tell a story, and the works of their hands tell a story— each thread connecting us to those who came before. And the story endures.
>
> Veronica Patterson
> *Piecework Magazine*

My Favorite Things

By Sandy Bonsib, 1997, Issaquah, Washington, 55" x 56"; appliqué shapes created by Cathy Sivesind and Sandy Bonsib; quilted by Becky Kraus. The appliqué shapes were inspired by some of my favorite things. I especially love animals, and our small farm includes one dog, three cats, six ducks, four goats, and several chickens.

Quilt for baby Cole Ryan Van Gerpen, made by Lynn Ahlers, Pam Keller, Karen Long, Linda Petrick, Cathy Sivesind, Kathy Staley, Kay Stotesbery, and Sandy Bonsib, 1998, Issaquah, Washington, 50" x 50".

MATERIALS: 42"-WIDE FABRIC

Fabric	Single Fabric	Scrappy/First Cut	Additional Cuts
A: Appliqué shapes Assorted colors	½ yd.	See step 1.	
B: Background squares Assorted blacks	¾ yd.	13 squares, 8" x 8"	
C: Triangles Assorted colors	1½ yds.	26 squares, 7" x 7"	◺
D: Sashing Multicolor stripe	¾ yd.	13 strips, 1¾" x 40"	18 pieces, 1¾" x 11½" 2 pieces, 1¾" x 14"
E: Side triangles Assorted plaids/stripes	⅔ yd.	2 squares, 20" x 20"	⊠ See Tip below.
F: Corner triangles Assorted plaids/stripes	½ yd.	2 squares, 13" x 13"	◹ See Tip below.
Backing	3⅓ yds.		
Binding (plaid)	⅔ yd.	6 strips, 2" x 40", cut on the bias	

Additional Supplies: Buttons for flower centers and moon's eye

Optional: pearl cotton, size 8, in assorted colors for finishing edges of appliqués and duck's eyes.

Optional: Chenille needle, size 24

TIP

If you want more variety in your corner and side triangles, make paper templates and cut individual triangles from assorted fabrics. Place the templates on the straight grain as indicated.

For side triangles, draw a 20" x 20" square on paper. Draw a line from corner to corner across both diagonals. Cut 1 of the triangles from the paper to use as a template.

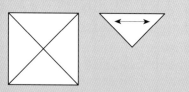

For corner triangles, draw a 13" x 13" square on paper. Draw a line from corner to corner. Cut 1 of the triangles from the paper to use as a template.

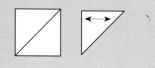

QUILT TOP ASSEMBLY

1. Using templates 1–10 (pages 105–7) and your favorite appliqué method, appliqué a shape to the center of each background square. If you fused the appliqués, secure the raw edges by hand or by machine with a blanket stitch (page 21).
2. Sew 4 Fabric C triangles to each appliquéd block, following the directions on page 23.

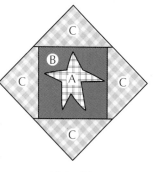

Make 13.

3. Trim each block to 11½" x 11½", centering the appliquéd square.
4. Arrange the blocks, short sashing strips, side triangles, and corner triangles as shown on page 38. Play with the arrangement until you are satisfied. Sew the blocks and short sashing strips into rows. Press the seam allowances toward the sashing.

5. Trim 2 Fabric D strips to 38½". Join 4 Fabric D strips end to end to make 1 long strip, then cut 2 strips, each 63" long. Join the rows and sashing strips, adding the corner triangles last. Press the seam allowances toward the sashing strips and triangles.

7. Layer the quilt top with batting and backing; baste. Quilt as desired. Bind the edges. Label your quilt.

8. Sew the buttons to the flower centers and to the moon for an eye. Make French knots for the duck's eyes.

French Knot

6. Trim the corner triangles even with the side triangles.

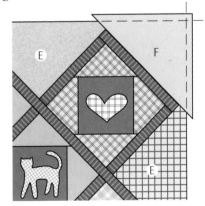

TRY IT ANOTHER WAY

Consider changing the appliqués. If you like dogs instead of cats, you can substitute! Refer to "Appliqué" on page 17 for ideas on creating your own appliqué shapes. If your shapes are too big or too small for the 8" squares, enlarge or reduce them with a copy machine.

Down on the Farm

By Sandy Bonsib, 1997, Issaquah, Washington, 49" x 83½"; quilted by Becky Kraus. Animals are favorite motifs in folk art. These wonderful woodcuts, including the mouse teasing the cat, are by Roger Bogers of Issaquah, Washington.

MATERIALS: 42"-WIDE FABRIC

Fabric	Single Fabric	Scrappy/First Cut
A: Center pieces		
Assorted light tans	1 yd.	11 pieces of varying sizes*
B: Courthouse Steps strips		
Assorted medium blacks/tans	½ yd.	10 strips, 1¼" x 40"
Assorted dark blacks	2½ yds.	70 strips, 1¼" x 40"
Outer Border		
Black-and-tan plaid	4 yds.**	6 strips, 8½" wide, cut on the bias (See Tip below.)
Backing	5 yds.	
Binding	½ yd.	7 strips, 2" x 40"

* The center pieces of my Courthouse Steps blocks vary in size from 5" x 6½"" to 10" x 11½". Because the size of the center pieces vary, so will the finished size of your quilt. For information about purchasing woodcuts on fabric, see page 101.

** For straight-grain borders, purchase 1¾ yards and cut 7 strips, 8½"" x 40".

TIP

Bias-cut borders often add just the right finishing touch to a quilt. To cut wide bias strips from large pieces of fabric, lay an ironed, single layer of fabric on a large table. Align the 45°-angle mark on a 6" x 24" ruler with the edge of the fabric, and draw a line along the ruler's edge as shown.

Using the first line as if it were a cut edge, draw a second line parallel to the first in the required width. (For strips wider than a 6" ruler, butt 2 rulers together.) Mark along the ruler's edge, moving the ruler as needed to reach the edge of the fabric.

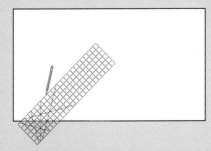

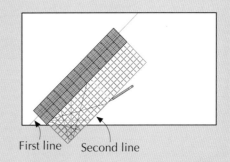

First line   Second line

When you reach the top of the ruler, move it halfway up the already marked line, maintaining the same angle. Draw along the edge of the ruler. Continue in this manner until you reach the fabric edge.

Cut on the lines. Be careful when handling the bias strips to avoid stretching the edges.

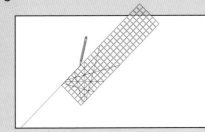

QUILT TOP ASSEMBLY

1. Using the Fabric A centers and Fabric B strips, make 10 Courthouse Steps blocks, following the directions on page 22. For each block, use dark fabrics for the first row, mediums for the second, and darks for each subsequent row. Use 5 strips on each side of small centers and 3 strips on each side of large centers.

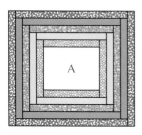 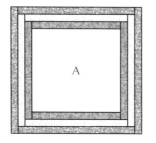

Block with small center   Block with large center

2. Arrange the blocks, 2 across and 5 down.
3. Working with 2 blocks at a time, add extra strips to the top or bottom of the smaller block until it is the same size as the larger block. You don't need to add strips symmetrically. For example, on the Farmer and the Plow block, I added 2 strips to the bottom only.

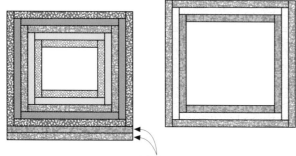

2 added strips

If the smaller block becomes larger than desired, trim the excess.

4. Sew the blocks together in horizontal rows.
5. Working with 2 rows, add extra strips to either or both sides of the smaller row until it is the width of the larger one. Again, you don't need to add strips symmetrically. On the Pig and Sheep row, I added 4 strips to the right side of the Sheep block only. If the smaller row becomes wider than desired, trim the excess.

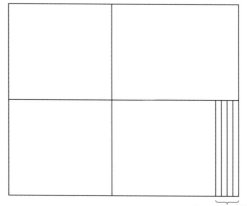

4 strips added

6. Join the rows to complete the quilt top.
7. Add the 8½"-wide border strips to the quilt top, referring to "Borders" on pages 28–29.
8. Layer the quilt top with batting and backing; baste. Quilt as desired. Bind the edges. Label your quilt.

TRY IT ANOTHER WAY

Use rubber stamps to embellish the center pieces of the Courthouse Steps blocks, or use a theme fabric.

Coffee or Tea?

By Sandy Bonsib, 1997, Issaquah, Washington, 42½" x 53"; quilted by Becky Kraus. This quilt is the last one I worked on for this book. Tired, and feeling like all my quilts looked the same, I asked my daughter Kate, age fourteen, and two of her friends—Rachel Richardson, twelve, and Melissa Richardson, ten—for help with the cups. Primitive folk-art shapes often look as though they were drawn by a child, and in this quilt, they were. Becky Kraus did a wonderful quilting job; she even included swirls of steam.

MATERIALS: 42"-WIDE FABRIC

Fabric	Single Fabric	Scrappy/First Cut
A: Appliqué shapes Assorted greens, reds, blacks	¾ yd.	See step 5.
B: Rail Fence Assorted medium & dark reds, blacks	1⅝ yds.	24 strips, 2¼" x 40"
C: Alternate squares Warm brown	1⅜ yds.	10 squares, 11" x 11"*
Backing	2¾ yds.	
Binding (plaid)	⅔ yd.	5 strips, 2" x 40", cut on the bias
Additional Supplies:	Optional: Black pearl cotton, size 8, for securing appliqué edges Optional: Chenille needle, size 24	
*See step 2.		

QUILT TOP ASSEMBLY

1. Join 6 Fabric B strips to make 1 strip set, arranging the strips from medium to dark. Make 4 strips sets. Cut a total of 10 squares, 11" x 11", from the strip sets. If the height of your strip set is not 11", adjust your cuts to the strip height so that you cut perfect squares. For example, if your strip set is only 10½" high, cut squares 10½" wide.

11"

11"

Make 4 strip sets.
Cut 10 squares.

2. From Fabric C, cut 10 squares, each 11" x 11", or the same size as the squares you cut from the strip sets.

3. Arrange the blocks as shown. Place the striped squares horizontally and vertically in alternate rows, with the darkest fabric on the bottom or right side. Sew the blocks together in horizontal rows.

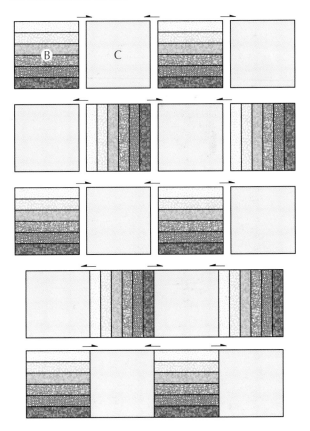

4. Join the rows.

5. Using templates 11–19 (pages 108–12) and your favorite appliqué method, make 15 coffee cups in assorted sizes and 2 saucers. Note that some cups are used both as shown and reversed. Plaids on the bias make interesting cups. Appliqué the cups and saucers to the quilt top, arranging some singly, some in horizontal rows, and stacking others as shown. Refer to the photo on page 42 for placement. If you fuse the shapes, secure the edges with a blanket stitch and black pearl cotton (see page 21).

6. Layer the quilt top with batting and backing; baste. Quilt as desired. On my quilt, large swirls of steam were quilted with tan thread so they would show against the dark background. You could also hand quilt the swirls with pearl cotton to make them stand out.

7. Bind the edges. Label your quilt.

TRY IT ANOTHER WAY

Using one of the cups, make place mats and a tea cozy—then invite your friends to tea!

All Plaids and Stripes

By Sandy Bonsib, 1997, Issaquah, Washington, 73½"x 61½"; machine quilted by Becky Kraus; hand stitched by Sandy Bonsib. Plaids and stripes add energy as well as a warm, homey feeling to quilts. I especially enjoy working with Roberta Horton's fabrics because of their colors and softness—all the plaids and stripes in this quilt are her designs.

MATERIALS: 42"-WIDE FABRIC

Fabric	Single Fabric	Scrappy/First Cut
A: Half-square triangle units Assorted light plaids & stripes	1¾ yds.	40 squares, 7½" x 7½"
Assorted medium & dark plaids & stripes	1¾ yds.	40 squares, 7½" x 7½"
B: Inner Border	¼ yd.	6 strips, 1" x 40"
C: Outer Border	1¼ yds.	6 strips, 6½" x 40"
D: Corner Squares	¼ yd.	4 squares, 6½" x 6½"
Backing	3¾ yds.	
Binding	½ yd.	7 strips 2" x 40", cut on the straight grain
Additional Supplies: Black pearl cotton, size 8 Chenille needle, size 24		

QUILT TOP ASSEMBLY

1. Pairing each Fabric A light square with a Fabric A medium or dark square, make 80 half-square triangle units, referring to "Method 2—Two for One" on page 24. Centering the diagonal line of an 8" Bias Square ruler on the seam line, trim each unit to 6½" x 6½".

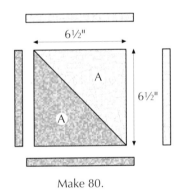

Make 80.

2. Arrange 4 half-square triangle units so the darker triangles form a diamond. Sew the units together to make a large block.

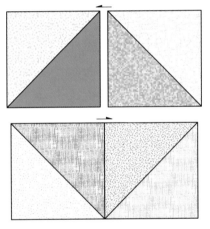

Make 20.

3. Place the blocks as shown below, playing with the arrangement until you are satisfied. Sew the blocks together in horizontal rows. Join the rows, matching the seams between the blocks.

4. Join 1"-wide inner border strips end to end. From the long strip, cut 2 pieces, each 48½" long, for the side borders, and 2 pieces, each 61½" long, for the top and bottom borders. Add the border strips to the sides of the quilt top first, then to the top and bottom edges. Refer to "Borders" on pages 28–29.

TIP

When sewing the inner border to the edge of your quilt top, sew with the wrong side of the quilt top up so you can see the X formed by the pieced triangles. Stitch through the center of the X to make sure the points on the triangles will not be cut off.

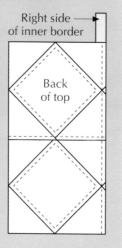

Right side of inner border

Back of top

5. Join the 6½"-wide outer border strips end to end. From the long strip, cut 2 pieces, each 61½" long, for the top and bottom borders, and 2 pieces, each 49½" long, for the side borders. Add the border strips, including corner squares, to the quilt top, referring to "Borders" on pages 28–29.

6. Layer the quilt top with batting and backing; baste. Quilt as desired.

7. Trace templates 4 and 20–23 (pages 106 and 112–14) onto the quilt top with a pencil or chalk; see the photo on page 45 for placement. Notice that the Chicken (template 20) is traced as shown and reversed. Use pearl cotton to sew a stem stitch along the traced lines. Make parallel lines between fence posts to create rails. Make French knots below the chicken's beaks for food.

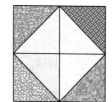

Stem Stitch

8. Bind the edges. Label your quilt.

TRY IT ANOTHER WAY

Place the light fabrics in the center of the diamonds. You'll be surprised at how different your quilt will look!

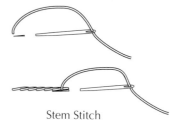

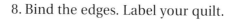

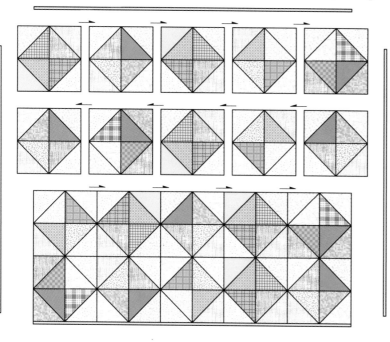

Only One Crow in the Garden

By Sandy Bonsib, 1997, Issaquah, Washington 53½" x 56"; quilted by Becky Kraus. Many quilters enjoy flowers and gardening almost as much as they enjoy quilting. This quilt was inspired by Roger Bogers's woodcut of flowers in a wheelbarrow (shown on facing page).

MATERIALS: 42"-WIDE FABRIC

Fabric	Single Fabric	Scrappy/First Cut
A: Flowers Assorted reds & golds	⅜ yd.	See step 2.
B: Crow Black	Scrap	See step 2.
C: Checkerboard Assorted medium & dark purples	1 yd.	15 strips, 2" x 40"
D: Checkerboard & background Tan-and-gray plaid	2¼ yds.	2 strips, 9½" x 45½", cut lengthwise 15 strips, 2" x 40", cut crosswise
E: Border Assorted reds	1 yd.	18 rectangles, 4½" x 10½" 2 rectangles, 4½" x 13½ "
Backing	3½ yds.	
Binding	½ yd.	6 strips, 2" x 40", cut on the straight grain
Additional Supplies:	Assorted buttons Optional: Pearl cotton, size 12, to match appliqué fabrics Optional: Sharp needle, size 8, 9, or 10	

QUILT TOP ASSEMBLY

1. Using the 2"-wide purple and background strips, make 150 Four Patch blocks as shown on page 21. I used 19 different purple fabrics, but the background fabric was the same in all the blocks.

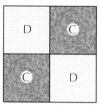

Make 150.

2. Using templates 24–32 (pages 114–16), trace 37 flowers in assorted sizes and 1 crow onto the paper side of lightweight, paper-backed fusible web. Following the manufacturer's directions, fuse the flowers to the wrong side of assorted red and gold fabrics. Fuse the crow to the wrong side of the black fabric. Cut out the pieces. Arrange the flowers and the crow on the two 45½" background pieces (see the photo on the facing page for placement). When you are satisfied with the arrangement, fuse them in place. Using thread to match the fabrics, outline the flowers and crow with a blanket stitch (see page 21). You can do this by hand or by machine.

3. To make the checkerboard pattern, arrange Four Patch blocks in rows of 15 blocks each. When arranging the Four Patch blocks, I placed darker ones at the top and bottom, brighter ones in the center. Play with the arrangement of the Four Patch blocks until you are satisfied. Join the rows to make 2 sections of 3 rows each and 1 section of 4 rows.

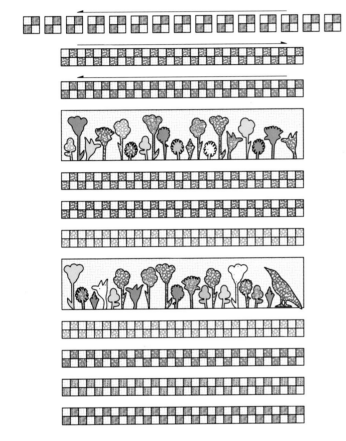

4. Join the Four Patch sections and the appliquéd background pieces. Press the seam allowances toward the appliquéd rows.

5. Arrange the border pieces around the edge of the quilt top. Use five 10½" pieces on each side, and four 10½" pieces and one 13½" piece on each of the top and bottom edges. Where two fabrics blend, rearrange. You want each fabric to be distinct even though they are all close in value.

6. Sew the side-border rectangles together, end to end. Trim the side borders to 48½", and sew them to the sides of the quilt top. Press the seam allowances toward the borders.

48½"

Side border
Make 2.

7. Sew together the rectangles for the top and bottom borders. They should not require trimming. Sew the borders to the quilt top.

8. Layer the quilt top with batting and backing; baste. Quilt as desired.

9. Bind the edges. Label your quilt.

10. Sew the buttons to the flower centers as desired.

TRY IT ANOTHER WAY

Too many flowers to appliqué? Select a few of your favorites and make pillows or a small wall hanging.

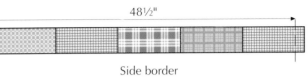

TIP

While making this quilt, I initially used a lot of gold for the flowers, with only a few reds. I discovered that it looked much better with almost as many reds as golds. Remember to add both bright and dark reds as well as bright and dark golds. The brights will give your quilt life.

Bickley & Bonsib

By Sandy Bonsib, 1993, Issaquah, Washington, 51½" x 88½"; machine quilted by Linda Kraus; hand quilted and hand stitched by Sandy Bonsib. Because I didn't change my name when my husband, John Bickley, and I married in 1980, we've always been known as "Bickley and Bonsib." The charms on one of the houses represent our son and daughter, and the cat represents our many animals.

MATERIALS: 42"-WIDE FABRIC

Fabric	Single Fabric	Scrappy/First Cut	Additional Cuts
A: Courthouse Steps centers Dark red	½ yd.	5 strips, 2½" x 40"	33 rectangles, 2½" x 5½"

B: Courthouse Steps logs
  Assorted med. reds, browns,
  golds & blacks
  Assorted light tans & off-whites
	3¼ yds.
	3¼ yds.
		75 strips, 1½" x 40"
		75 strips, 1½" x 40"	

C: Background for houses Assorted light tans	⅜ yd.	3 rectangles, 8½" x 11½"	

D, E, F: Houses
  Assorted med. & dark reds,
  browns & blacks
	¼ yd.	See step 2.	

G: Inner Border Medium red	½ yd.	7 strips, 2" x 40"	
H: Outer Border Light tan	1½ yds.	2 strips, 10" x 51½", cut lengthwise	
I: Letters Gray	1 yd.	8 to 10 strips, 1⅜" wide cut on the bias	
Backing	5½ yds.		
Binding	½ yd.	8 strips, 2" x 40"	

Additional Supplies: About 100 buttons of assorted sizes: off-white, gray, and black
Black and gray pearl cotton, size 8
Chenille needle, size 24
Optional: charms: 1 boy, 1 girl, 1 cat

QUILT TOP ASSEMBLY

1. Using the Fabric A centers and 1½"-wide Fabric B strips, make 33 Courthouse Steps blocks, following the directions on page 22, but add strips to the sides of the center piece first rather than to the top and bottom. Sew 3 strips to each side of the centers, placing lights on the short sides and mediums and darks on the long sides.

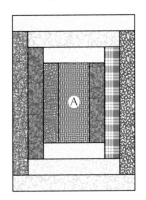

Make 33.

2. Using templates 33–36 (page 117) and your favorite appliqué method, appliqué the houses to the Fabric C rectangles.

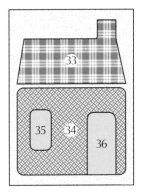

Make 3.

3. Arrange the blocks, placing the rectangle centers vertically as shown. Play with the arrangement until you are satisfied. Place brighter fabrics asymmetrically throughout the top.

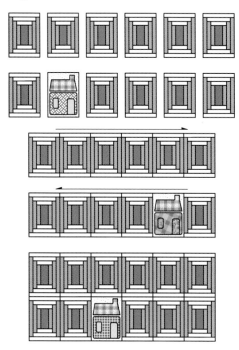

4. Sew the blocks together in horizontal rows. Join the rows, matching the seams between the blocks.

5. Join the 2"-wide inner border strips end to end. From the long strip, cut 2 pieces, each 48½" long, for the top and bottom borders, and 2 pieces, each 69½" long, for the sides. Add the inner border strips to the top and bottom edges first, then to the sides.

6. Add the 10"-wide outer border strips to the top and bottom edges. Press the seam allowances toward the inner borders.

7. Layer the quilt top with batting and backing; baste. Quilt as desired.

8. Sew a running stitch around the appliquéd houses and inside the doors and windows, using pearl cotton.

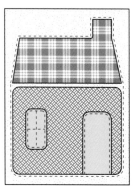

9. Use Fabric I bias strips to make bias tubes for the letters and numbers, following the directions on page 25. Use chalk or a pencil to draw the appropriate names and dates on the outer border strips. Notice that in the quilt shown on page 51, the letters and numbers are different sizes and are not placed in a straight line. Cut bias tubes as needed for the letters and fix in place with a gluestick.

TIP

To center your letters, first write the word(s) you plan to use on paper. Then find the half-way point and place that letter in the middle of your quilt border. Place the rest of the letters to the right and left. For letters placed to the left, I refer to the word on paper so that when I'm spelling it backwards (as I work to the left of the center), I don't misspell it.

10. Sew along the center of the bias tubes with a running stitch, using pearl cotton that matches the fabric (see page 25). Appliqué around tight curves so they don't curl up. I made the "ampersand" for "Bickley & Bonsib" with a running stitch, using a double strand of pearl cotton.

11. Add buttons for smoke from the chimneys. See the photo on page 51 for placement. Notice that the buttons become smaller as the smoke curls up. I also changed the colors of the buttons as they swirled upward, putting dark buttons on light fabric and light buttons on dark fabric so the smoke would show. I also used a button for the period after "EST."

12. Sew charms on one house, if desired. I have a son, a daughter, and many animals, which is why I chose boy, girl, and cat charms. Choose your charms to fit your family.

13. Bind the edges. Label your quilt.

TRY IT ANOTHER WAY

Use first names, such as "John & Lynn," or your last name, such as "Taylor Family." Include a date that is special to you or your family.

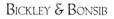

Quilted Clouds

By Sandy Bonsib, 1997, Issaquah, Washington, 50½" x 41½"; quilted by Becky Kraus. Living in the Seattle area, I've learned to love cloudy days. They're a wonderful excuse to stay inside and make a quilt! The clouds are like a quilt covering the earth. The small buttons represent the sun's rays peeking through. If you look carefully, you can see machine-quilted geese flying through the clouds.

MATERIALS: 42"-WIDE FABRIC

	Single Fabric	Scrappy/First Cut	Additional Cuts
GOOSE TRACKS BLOCKS			
Assorted light tans	1¼ yds.		
A		48 rectangles, 2½" x 4½"	
B		24 squares, 3¼" x 3¼"	⊠
C		48 squares, 2½" x 2½"	
D		1 square, 10½" x 10½"	
Assorted dark tans	⅞ yd.		
E		24 squares, 4⅞" x 4⅞"	◿
F		24 squares, 3¼" x 3¼"	⊠
G		12 squares, 2½" x 2½"	
STRIPS OF SMALL SQUARES			
H: Assorted light tans	¼ yd.	71 squares, 1½" x 1½"	
FOUR PATCH BLOCKS			
I: Light tan	¼ yd.	2 strips, 2½" x 40"	
J: Medium brown	¼ yd.	2 strips, 2½" x 40"	
FLYING GEESE BLOCKS			
K: Medium-light tan	⅔ yd.	66 squares, 3" x 3"	
		1 rectangle, 1½" x 5½"	
L: Assorted light & medium tans	⅝ yd.	33 rectangles, 3" x 5½"	
M: Bottom border			
Medium brown plaid	1⅔ yds.	1 strip, 5½" x 45½", cut on the bias	
Head, hand	Scraps	See step 12.	
Woman's dress	¼ yd.	See step 12.	
Watering can	Scrap	See step 12.	
Backing	2¾ yds.		
Binding (plaid)	⅔ yd.	5 strips, 2" x 40", cut on the bias	

Additional Supplies: 3-ply jute for hair
Maroon, black, and brown pearl cotton, size 8
Chenille needle, size 24
8 buttons for flowers
Assorted small off-white buttons
10½" square of lightweight interfacing

QUILT TOP ASSEMBLY

1. Make 12 Goose Tracks blocks, following the directions on page 22, using Fabrics A through C and E through G.

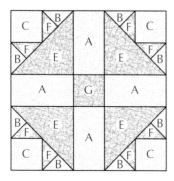

Make 12.

2. Join assorted light tan squares (Fabric H) to make 2 rows of small squares, one with 30 squares, the other with 41 squares.

3. Make 9 Four Patch blocks, following the directions on page 21, using Fabrics I and J.

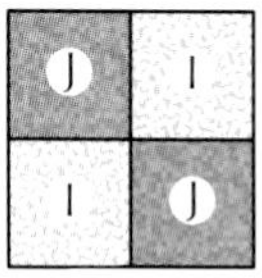

Make 9.

4. Make 33 Flying Geese blocks, following the directions on page 21, using Fabrics K and L.

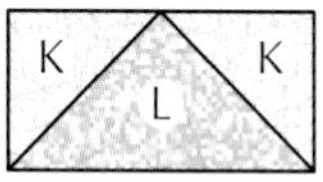

Make 33.

5. Arrange 11 of the Goose Tracks blocks and the 10½" Fabric D square as shown. Sew the blocks together in horizontal rows. Join the rows, matching the seams between the blocks.

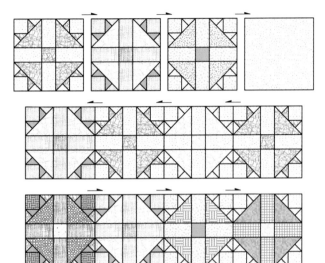

6. Sew the row of 30 Fabric H squares to the right side of the Goose Track blocks. Sew the row of 41 Fabric H squares to the upper edge.

7. Join 16 Flying Geese blocks and the Fabric K rectangle to make the top border. Join 17 Flying Geese Blocks to make the right border, and trim 1½" from the bottom of the row.

1½" x 5½"

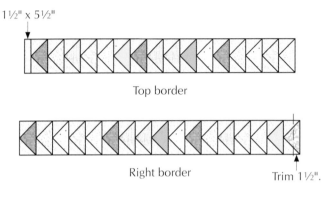

Top border

Right border   Trim 1½".

8. Referring to the illustration below, sew the top border of Flying Geese blocks to the top edge of the quilt top.

9. Join 9 Four Patch blocks to make the left border. Sew this to the left side of the quilt.

10. Sew the Fabric M piece to the bottom of the quilt.

11. Sew the remaining row of Flying Geese blocks to the right side of the quilt.

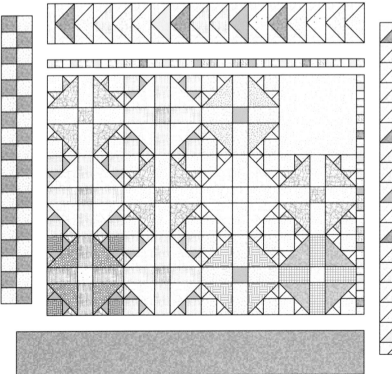
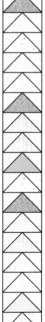

12. Using templates 37–40 (pages 118–19) and your favorite appliqué method, appliqué the woman's dress, head, hand, and watering can. Refer to the quilt on page 54 for placement.

13. With right sides together, sew the remaining Goose Tracks block to the 10½" square of lightweight interfacing. Slit the interfacing and turn the block right side out; press. Appliqué the block on point to the upper right corner of the quilt top.
14. Layer the quilt top with batting and backing; baste. Quilt as desired.
15. Bind the edges. Label your quilt.

16. For the woman's hair, gather the jute at one end to form bangs and separate the plies to form the rest of the hair. Gather it with maroon pearl cotton to form a ponytail. Arrange the jute so that it covers the back of the woman's head. Stitch the jute to the quilt top.
17. Make a French knot for the woman's eye with black pearl cotton.
18. Using brown pearl cotton, stitch stems for the flowers. Attach the button flowers with pearl cotton. Using a running stitch and brown pearl cotton, stitch water pouring from the watering can.
19. Sew small buttons randomly around the appliquéd Goose Tracks block.

TRY IT ANOTHER WAY

Try another color, such as light blues, for the "sky" of Goose Tracks blocks, rows of Small Squares, Flying Geese blocks, and Four Patch blocks.

Color Me Bright

By Sandy Bonsib, 1996, Issaquah, Washington; quilted by Becky Kraus. I teach quiltmaking classes, and one of the blocks my students make in the intermediate class is the Album Patch. It's a traditional design and is often used as a friendship block. The addition of bright plaids, made by Sharon Yenter for In The Beginning Fabrics, proved to be just the right touch for the borders.

MATERIALS: 42"-WIDE FABRIC

Fabric	Single Fabric	Scrappy/First Cut	Additional Cuts
ALBUM PATCH			
A: Assorted colors	1 yd.	36 squares, 2⅝" x 2⅝"	cut only 18 squares ◻
		9 rectangles, 2⅝" x 6⅞"	
		27 squares, 4½" x 4½"	⊠
B: Assorted colors	½ yd.	72 squares, 2⅝" x 2⅝"	
C: Assorted colors	¾ yd.	36 rectangles, 2⅝" x 6⅞"	
D: Inner Border Plaids	½ yd.*	4 strips, 3½" x 36½"	
E: Purple corner squares	⅛ yd.	4 squares, 3½" x 3½"	
F: Middle Border Assorted colors	½ yd.	128 squares, 1¾" x 1¾"	
		6 rectangles, 1¾" x 2"	
		4 rectangles, 1½" x 1¾"	
G: Outer Border Plaids	1⅜ yds.*	4 strips, 4½" x 45", cut lengthwise	
H: Red corner squares	¼ yd.	4 squares, 4½" x 4½"	
Backing	3¼ yds.		
Binding	½ yd.	6 strips, 2" x 40", cut on the straight grain	

Additional Supplies: Assorted colorful buttons

* On my quilt, I cut each border strip from a different fabric. If you want to do this, you need ⅛ yard each of 4 fabrics for the first border (cut crosswise) and 1⅜ yards each of 4 fabrics for the third border (cut lengthwise). Cut 1 strip from each fabric. You will have plenty of leftover fabric for other projects.

QUILT TOP ASSEMBLY

1. Using Fabrics A, B, and C, make 12 Album Patch blocks, following the directions on page 23. The side and corner triangles are oversized. Trim the blocks to 12½" x 12½", leaving a ¼" seam allowance beyond the points.

2. Arrange the blocks as shown.

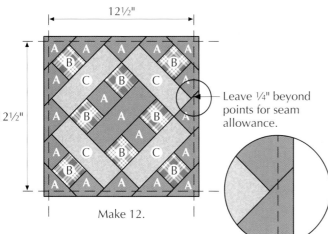

Make 12.

Leave ¼" beyond points for seam allowance.

3. Sew the blocks together in horizontal rows. Join the rows, matching seams between the blocks.

4. Add the 3½"-wide inner border, including the Fabric E corner squares, to the quilt top, referring to "Borders" on pages 28–29.

5. For the middle borders, join Fabric F pieces as follows, placing rectangles randonly:

    30 squares (1¾" x 1¾") and 3 rectangles (1¾" x 2") for each of the side borders

    34 squares (1¾" x 1¾") and 2 rectangles (1½" x 1¾") for each of the top and bottom borders

6. Sew the short rows of squares to the sides of the quilt top, then sew the remaining rows to the top and bottom edges.

TRY IT ANOTHER WAY

The Album Patch block lends itself to projects of all sizes. A few blocks would make a table runner and many blocks would make a beautiful bed quilt.

Album Patch is a wonderful friendship or signature block. Just use light values for the Fabric A rectangles so you can write or stitch your name, date, or favorite saying on them.

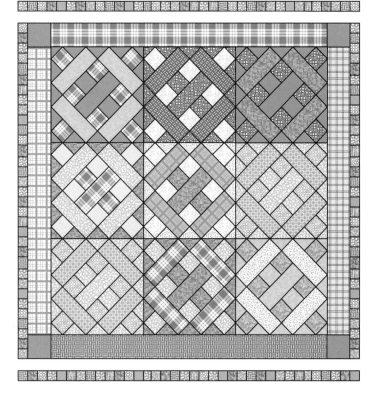

7. Add the 4½"-wide outer borders, including the Fabric H corner squares, to the quilt top, referring to "Borders" on pages 28–29.

8. Layer the quilt top with batting and backing; baste. Quilt as desired. Bind the edges. Label your quilt.

9. Sew buttons randomly to the squares in the middle border.

... But Keep the Old

By Sandy Bonsib, 1997, Issaquah, Washington, 66" x 60½"; made in friendship by Lynn Ahlers, Pam Keller, Karen Long, Linda Petrick, Cathy Sivesind, Kathy Staley, Kay Stotesbery, and Sue Van Gerpen; heart buttons made by Kathy Staley; quilted by Becky Kraus. I belong to a group of quilters who love folk art. We call ourselves the Flannel Folks and Button Babes, and each month we exchange simple blocks. In one of our more ambitious moments, we decided to make and exchange Heart blocks. These blocks were made in my chosen colors of red and brown. Notice the placement of the *s* in *friends*. This is an example of a planned mistake.

MATERIALS: 42"-WIDE FABRIC

Fabric	Single Fabric	Scrappy/First Cut	Additional Cuts
LARGE HEARTS			
A: Assorted reds	1¼ yds.	116 squares, 3½" x 3½"	
B: Assorted browns	1 yd.	80 squares, 3½" x 3½"	
A: Assorted browns	¼ yd.	14 squares, 3½" x 3½"	
B: Assorted reds	⅛ yd.	10 squares, 3½" x 3½"	
C: 9 assorted reds & browns	¼ yd. each	See step 4.	
SMALL HEARTS			
D: Assorted golds	¼ yd.	12 squares, 2" x 2"	
E. Assorted browns	½ yd.	8 squares, 4" x 4"	
		4 squares, 2" x 2"	
		8 rectangles, 1⅛" x 3½"	
		4 rectangles, 1¾" x 5½"	
		4 rectangles, 1¼" x 5½"	
PINWHEELS			
F: Assorted reds	¼ yd.	18 squares, 3⅜" x 3⅜"	
G: Assorted browns	¼ yd.	18 squares, 3⅜" x 3⅜"	
H & I: Letters Assorted reds & golds	¾ yd.	425 squares, 1½" x 1½"	
J: Extra pieces Assorted browns	¼ yd.	1 rectangle, 3½" x 16"	
		1 rectangle, 4½" x 6½"	
K: Borders Gold-and-brown plaid	1¼ yds.	6 strips, 5½" x 40"	
Backing	4 yds.		
Binding Assorted browns	½ yd.	28 pieces, 2" x 10", cut on the straight grain	

Additional Supplies: 40 assorted heart-shaped buttons

QUILT TOP ASSEMBLY

Large Hearts

1. To make red Hearts 1, 2, 4–6, 8, and 9, select 14 red squares for each heart and 10 brown squares for each background. To make red Heart 7, select an additional 4 red squares to make a larger heart.

    Using 8 squares of each color, make 8 half-square triangle units, referring to "Method 1—Sew and Flip" on page 24. Arrange 6 red squares, 2 brown squares, and 8 half-square triangle units as shown for each heart except heart 7; for that heart, use 10 red squares, 2 brown squares, and 8 half-square triangle units. Sew the squares and half-square triangle units in rows, then join the rows.

2. Make brown Heart 3 as described in step 1. Use 14 brown squares for the heart and 10 red squares for the background.

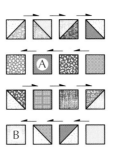

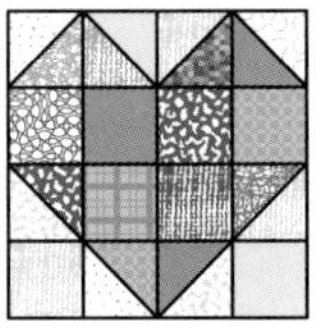

Make 7 red hearts.
Make 1 brown heart.

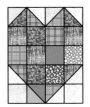

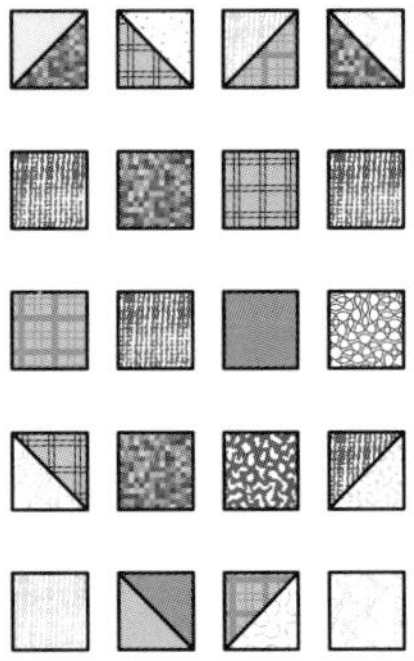

Heart #7
Make 1 red heart.

3. To trim the Heart blocks, cut 1½" from the upper edge and ¼" from each side. Do not trim the bottom edge. Heart blocks 1–6, 8, and 9 should measure 12" x 11", including seam allowances. Heart block 7 should measure 12" x 14".

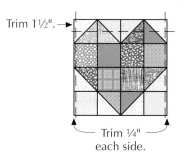

Trim 1½".

Trim ¼" each side.

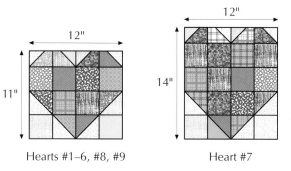

Hearts #1–6, #8, #9   Heart #7

12"

11"

12"

14"

4. Cut 4 strips for each heart from the same fabric (Fabric C) as follows:

Hearts 1, 8, and 9   2 strips, 2½" x 11"
    1 strip, 2½" x 16"
    1 strip, 3" x 16"

Hearts 2 and 3   2 strips, 2½" x 11"
    1 strip, 2½" x 16"
    1 strip, 3½" x 16"

Hearts 4, 5, and 6   2 strips, 2½" x 11"
    2 strips, 2½" x 16"

Heart 7   2 strips, 2½" x 14"
    2 strips, 2½" x 16"

Sew the strips to the sides first, then to the top and bottom edges. Press the seam allowances toward the strips.

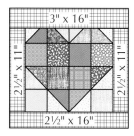

Heart #1

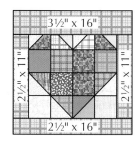

Hearts #2, #3

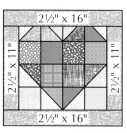

Hearts #4, #5, #6

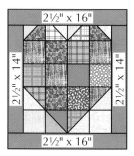

Heart #7

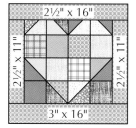

Hearts #8, #9

Small Hearts

1. Make a Four Patch Block, using 3 gold (Fabric D) 2" squares, and 1 brown (Fabric E) 2" square.

Make 4.

2. Sew 2 brown (Fabric E) half-square triangles to opposite sides of each Four Patch block, trimming excess as shown. To center the triangles, align each triangle's point with the seam in the Four Patch block. Sew triangles to the remaining 2 sides of each block.

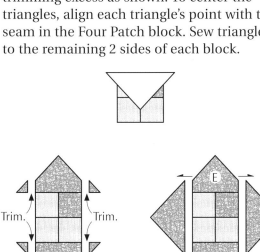

3. Trim the top and sides along the points of the heart as shown. Trim the bottom, leaving a ¼" seam allowance below the point of the heart.

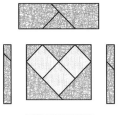

4. Sew a 3½" Fabric E rectangle to each side of each small heart. Sew the 1¾" x 5½" Fabric E rectangles to the top edges, and the 1¼" x 5½" Fabric E rectangles to the bottom edges. The small Heart blocks should measure 5½" x 5½", including seam allowances.

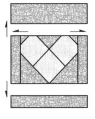

5. Trim one of the small hearts to 4½" x 5½" as shown. This heart will be on its side above the word *friends*.

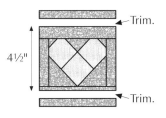

Pinwheel Blocks

Using 18 red (Fabric F) and 18 brown (Fabric G) 3⅜" squares, make 36 half-square triangle units. Refer to "Method 2—Two for One" on page 24. Join the half-square triangle units as shown.

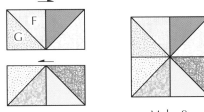

Make 9.

Pieced Letters

Make the pieced letters, using Fabrics H and I, following the directions on page 26. Join the letters to make words, adding rows of squares above, between, and below the letters as shown. Do not add the *s* to *friends*; you'll add it later to the right border.

Joining the Blocks

1. Arrange the blocks, including the extra pieces, as shown. Join the blocks.

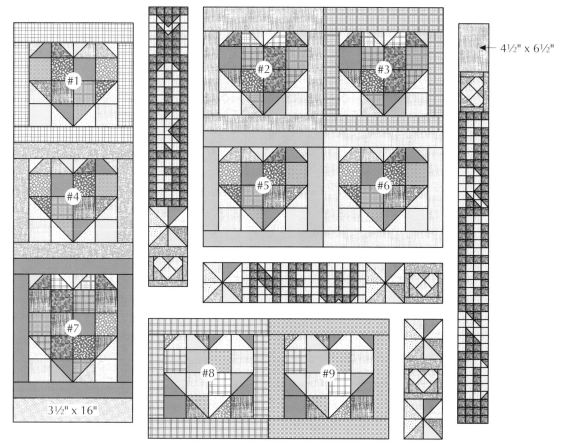

4½" x 6½"

3½" x 16"

2. Join the 5½"-wide border strips end to end. From the long strip, cut 2 pieces, each 56" long, for the top and bottom borders. Cut 1 piece, 50½" long, for the left border. Cut 1 piece, 45½" long, for the right border.

3. Add the s to the bottom of the right border and sew the border to the right edge of the quilt top. Sew the left border to the left edge. Press the seam allowances toward the border strips. Sew a Pinwheel block to each end of the remaining border strips, then sew them to the top and bottom edges.

4. Layer the quilt top with batting and backing; baste. Quilt as desired. Cut the binding strips into 10"-long pieces. Join them end to end, then bind the edges. Label your quilt.

5. Sew the heart-shaped buttons randomly on the borders.

TRY IT ANOTHER WAY

Using small Heart blocks and alternate plain squares, make pillows or a small wall hanging to go with your quilt.

A Duck with Lips and His Friends

By Sandy Bonsib, 1997, Issaquah, Washington, 37½" x 53½"; quilted by Becky Kraus. If the duck's beak really looks like lips, I guess I need to work on it some more. Originally inspired by a half-square triangle unit made into a chicken by Cathy Sivesind, I decided to try making the whole farm! Everyone has a favorite. Which one is yours?

More Friends

By Sandy Bonsib, 1997, Issaquah, Washington, 37½" x 53½"; quilted by Becky Kraus. Once I started making animals, I couldn't stop. So the Duck with Lips has even more friends.

MATERIALS: 42"-WIDE FABRIC

You need ¼ yard for the background of each animal.
Use scraps for the animal body parts.

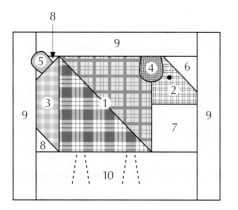

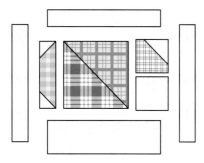

SHEEP		
	Piece No.	Amount & Size
Body	1	2 squares, 4½" x 4½"
Head	2	1 square, 2½" x 2½"
Rear	3	1 rectangle, 1½" x 4½"
Ear	4	Template 48
Tail	5	1 rectangle, 1" x 3"
Background	6	1 square, 2" x 2"
	7	1 square, 2½" x 2½"
	8	2 squares, 1½" x 1½"
	9	3 rectangles, 1½" x 7½"
	10	1 rectangle, 2½" x 7½"
Eye	1 button	
Legs	Stitched	

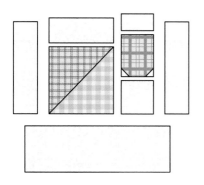

COW		
	Piece No.	Amount & Size
Body	1	2 squares, 4½" x 4½"
Head	2	1 rectangle, 2½" x 3"
Background	3	2 squares, 1" x 1"
	4	2 rectangles, 2" x 6"
	5	1 rectangle, 3¼" x 9½"
	6	1 rectangle, 1½" x 2½"
	7	1 square, 2½" x 2½"
	8	1 rectangle 2" x 4½"
Ear	9	Template 41
Eyes	2 buttons	
Legs & tail	Stitched	

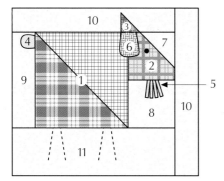

GOAT		
	Piece No.	Amount & Size
Body	1	2 squares, 4½" x 4½"
Head	2	1 square, 2½" x 2½"
Horn	3	1 square, 3" x 3"
Tail	4	1 rectangle, 1" x 2"
Beard	5	4 rectangles, ½" x 2"
Ear	6	Template 41
Background	7	1 square, 2" x 2"
	8	1 square, 2½" x 2½"
	9	1 rectangle, 1½" x 4½"
	10	2 rectangles, 1½" x 7½"
	11	1 rectangle, 2½" x 7½"
Eye	1 button	
Legs	Stitched	

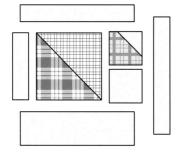

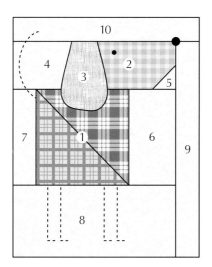

DOG		
	Piece No.	Amount & Size
Body	1	2 squares, 4½" x 4½"
Head	2	1 rectangle, 2½" x 4½"
Ear	3	Template 42
Background	4	1 rectangle, 2½" x 3½"
	5	1 square, 1½" x 1½"
	6	1 rectangle, 2½" x 4½"
	7	1 rectangle, 1½" x 4½"
	8	1 rectangle, 3½" x 7½"
	9	1 rectangle, 1½" x 9½"
	10	1 rectangle, 1½" x 8½"
Nose	1 button	
Tail & legs	Stitched	

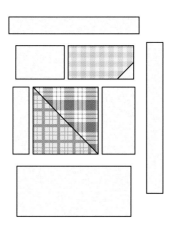

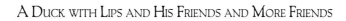

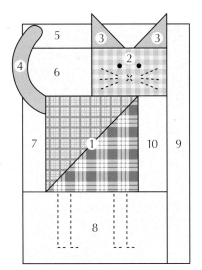

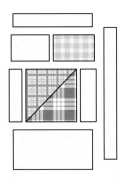

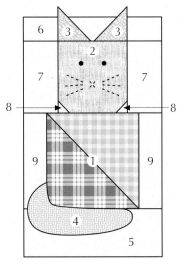

WALKING CAT		
	Piece No.	Amount & Size
Body	1	2 squares, 4½" x 4½"
Head	2	1 rectangle, 2½" x 3¾"
Ears	3	2 squares, 3" x 3"
Tail	4	Template 43
Background	5	1 rectangle, 1½" x 6¾"
	6	1 rectangle, 2½" x 3½"
	7	1 rectangle, 1½" x 4½"
	8	1 rectangle, 3½" x 6¾"
	9	1 rectangle, 1½" x 10½"
	10	1 rectangle, 1¾" x 4½"
Eyes	2 buttons	
Nose, whiskers & legs	Stitched	

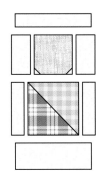

SITTING CAT		
	Piece No.	Amount & Size
Body	1	2 squares, 4½" x 4½"
Head	2	1 square, 3½" x 3½"
Ears	3	2 squares, 3" x 3"
Tail	4	Template 44
Background	5	1 rectangle, 2½" x 6½"
	6	1 rectangle, 1½" x 6½"
	7	2 rectangles, 2" x 3½"
	8	2 squares, 1" x 1"
	9	2 rectangles, 1½" x 4½"
Eyes	2 buttons	
Nose, whiskers, legs & edges of tail	Stitched	

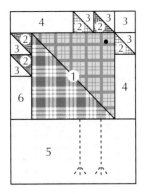

Chicken 1

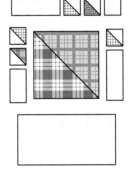

Chicken 2

CHICKEN (1 & 2)		
	Piece No.	Amount & Size
Body	1	2 squares, 4½" x 4½"
Tail, comb & beak	2	5 squares, 1½" x 1½"
Background	3	6 squares, 1½" x 1½"
	4	2 rectangles, 1½" x 3½"
	5	1 rectangle, 3½" x 6½"
	6	1 rectangle, 1½" x 2½"
Eye	1 button	
Legs (Chicken 1)	Stitched	
Nest (Chicken 2)	5 selvages or ½" strips	
Eggs (Chicken 2)	3 buttons	

HORSE		
	Piece No.	Amount & Size
Body	1	2 squares, 4½" x 4½"
Neck	2	1 rectangle, 1½" x 2½"
Head	3	1 rectangle, 2½" x 3½"
Ear	4	1 square, 2½" x 2½"
Background	5	3 rectangles, 1½" x 8½"
	6	1 rectangle, 3½" x 4½"
	7	1 square, 1" x 1"
	8	1 rectangle, 2½" x 6½"
	9	1 rectangle, 3½" x 8½"
Eye	1 button	
Mane, tail & legs	Stitched	

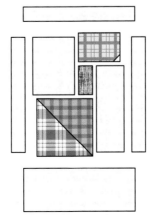

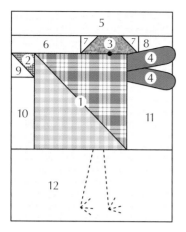

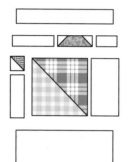

DUCK WITH LIPS		
	Piece No.	Amount & Size
Body	1	2 squares, 4½" x 4½"
Tail	2	1 square, 1½" x 1½"
Head	3	1 rectangle, 1¼" x 3"
Lips (beak)	4	2 of Template 45
Background	5	1 rectangle, 1½" x 7½"
	6	1 rectangle, 1¼" x 3½"
	7	2 squares, 1¼" x 1¼"
	8	1 rectangle, 1¼" x 2"
	9	1 square, 1½" x 1½"
	10	1 rectangle, 1½" x 3½"
	11	1 rectangle, 2½" x 4½"
	12	1 rectangle, 3½" x 7½"
Feet	Stitched	
Eye	1 button	

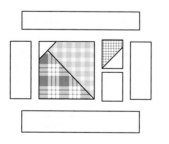

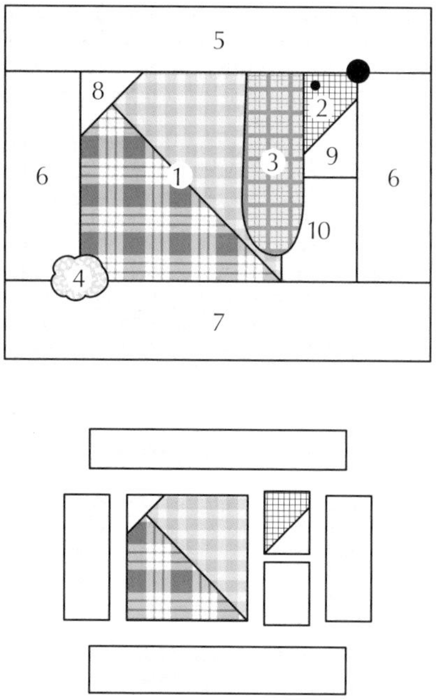

RABBIT		
	Piece No.	Amount & Size
Body	1	2 squares, 4½" x 4½"
Head	2	1 rectangle, 2" x 2½"
Ear	3	Template 46
Tail	4	Template 47 (fused)
Background	5	1 rectangle, 1¾" x 9"
	6	2 rectangles, 2" x 4½"
	7	1 rectangle, 2" x 9"
	8	1 square, 1¾" x 1¾"
	9	1 square, 2" x 2"
	10	1 rectangle, 2" x 2½"
Eye	Stitched	
Nose	1 button	

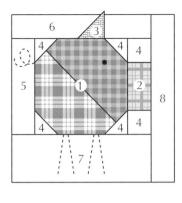

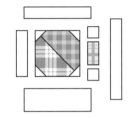

PIG		
	Piece No.	Amount & Size
Body	1	2 squares, 4½" x 4½"
Snout	2	1 rectangle, 1½" x 2½"
Ear	3	1 square, 3" x 3"
Background	4	6 squares, 1½" x 1½"
	5	1 rectangle, 1½" x 4½"
	6	1 rectangle, 1½" x 6½"
	7	1 rectangle, 2½" x 6½"
	8	1 rectangle, 1½" x 7½"
Eye	1 button	
Tail & legs	Stitched	

Fabric	Single Fabric	Scrappy/First Cut
Assorted Strips (each quilt)	1½ yds.	48 pieces, 1½" to 2½" x 20"
Assorted Squares (each quilt)	⅔ yd.	263 squares, 1½" x 1½"
Inner Border (each quilt)	⅓ yd.	4 strips, 2" x 40"
Outer Border (each quilt)	¾ yd.	5 strips, 4½" x 40"
Corner Blocks (Quilt 2) Assorted squares	¼ yd.	64 squares, 1½" x 1½"
Backing (each quilt)	1¾ yds.	
Binding (Quilt 1)	⅔ yd.	200" pieced from 2"-wide bias strips
Binding (Quilt 2)	⅓ yd.	5 strips, 2" x 40", cut on the straight grain

Additional Supplies: Black pearl cotton, size 8
Chenille needle, size 24

QUILT TOP ASSEMBLY

1. Choose 6 Animal blocks and assemble them, following the piecing diagrams. Block sizes will vary.

   To make half-square triangle units, use "Method 1—Sew and Flip" on page 24.

   To add triangle corners (for example, pieces 2 and 6 in the sheep), draw a diagonal line on the wrong side of the small square. Place it on the appropriate corner of the larger piece. Sew on the diagonal line, trim the seam allowance to ¼" and press the triangle toward the corner.

   Use templates 41–48 (pages 119–20) for three-dimensional ears and tails, *adding seam allowances before cutting*. Sew and turn the pieces; fold ears for cow, sheep, goat, and rabbit. Do not fold dog ear and cat tails. Fold

squares as shown for horse, pig, and cat ears, and for goat horn. Insert pieces before stitching seams.

Sew; clip curves.

Turn.

Fold ears for dog, cow, sheep, goat, and rabbit.

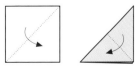

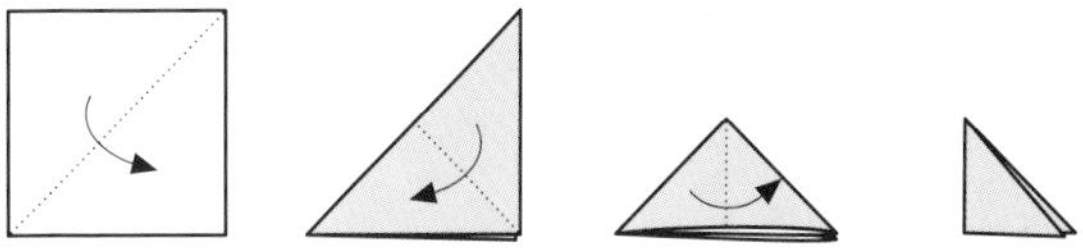

Ears for cat, horse, and pig; horn for goat

2. Using the assorted strips, sew 1 strip to the left and lower edges of each animal and 3 strips each to the right and upper edges as shown. Block sizes will vary. Pin ears and tails out of the way when adding strips.

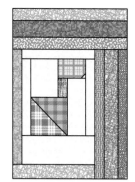

3. Arrange the Animal blocks as desired, 2 across and 3 down.

4. Measure the width of the Animal blocks. They all need to be 13½" wide. Add strips of joined 1½" squares to either the right or left sides until each block is 13½" or wider. If wider, trim the excess.

13½"

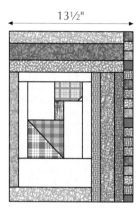

5. Sew the blocks together in vertical rows. Add strips of joined 1½" squares to the top or bottom of the rows as needed until they are the same length.

6. Join the rows.
7. Referring to "Borders" on pages 28–29, measure and add inner borders to the quilt top. For the outer border of Quilt 1, measure and add borders, including corner squares. For the outer border of Quilt 2, measure and add borders.

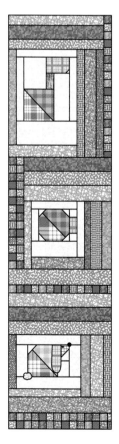

8. Layer the quilt top with batting and backing; baste. Quilt as desired. Bind the edges of Quilt 1 with bias strips. Bind the edges of Quilt 2 with strips cut on the straight grain. Label your quilt.
9. For the animals, use a running stitch to embroider legs and whiskers, and make French knots for eyes or use buttons.

TRY IT ANOTHER WAY

Choose your favorite Animal block and, placing it askew, appliqué it near the open edge of a pillowcase.

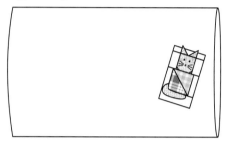

Choose your favorite Animal block, for example, the Horse. Make three or four Horse blocks. If you feel creative, you can even experiment with changing the size of the block, so it looks like you have a mother and babies. Place the blocks in a row to make a small quilt or wall hanging.

These blocks do not need to turn out a particular size. If your blocks are different in width than mine and you don't wish to add to them or trim them down, adjust the borders to fit the dimensions of your quilt top.

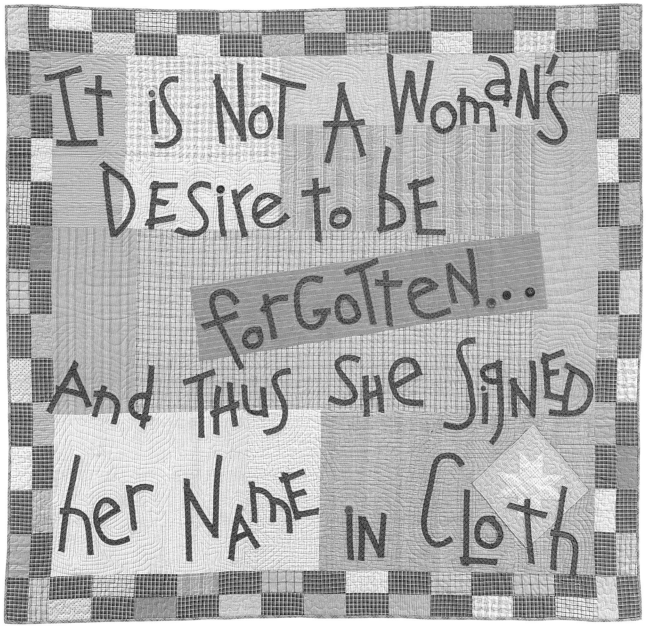

By Sandy Bonsib, 1997, Issaquah, Washington, 60½" x 56½"; quilted by Becky Kraus. I used one of my favorite quotations for this quilt, from the book *Remember Me* by Linda Otto Lipsett. Many quilts that have been passed down through generations aren't identified with their maker's name. As with most folk art objects, the quilts were never expected to become treasures cherished by later generations. This quilt is beautifully machine quilted with echo quilting, echoing, in a way, the voices of the many quiltmakers who came before us.

Materials: 42"-wide Fabric

Fabric	Single Fabric	Scrappy/First Cut
A: LETTERS		
A: Dark red	2½ yds.	Approximately 360" of bias strips, cut 1⅜" wide
B: Background Assorted blues	1¾ yds.	(1) 7½" x 16½" (2) 10½" x 15½" (3) 6½" x 15½" (4) 7½" x 24½" (5) 9½" x 24½" (6) 8½" x 17½" (7) 17½" x 38½" (8) 5½" x 6½" (9) 6½" x 28½" (10) 15½" x 18½" (11) 7½" x 15½" (12) 15½" x 27½" (13) 7½" x 33½"
STAR		
C: Light tan	¼ yd.	1 square, 3½" x 3½" 8 squares, 2" x 2"
D: Light blue	¼ yd.	4 rectangles, 2" x 3½" 4 squares, 2" x 2" 2 rectangles, 1½" x 6½" 2 rectangles, 1½" x 8½"
BORDER		
E: Assorted light blues	¾ yd.	8 strips, 2½" x 40"
F: Assorted medium blues	¾ yd.	8 strips, 2½" x 40"
Backing	3½ yds.	
Binding (plaid)	1 yd.	6 strips, 2" x 40", cut on the bias

Additional Supplies: Dark red and black pearl cotton, size 8
Chenille needle, size 24
7 assorted buttons
Gluestick
8½" square of lightweight interfacing

Quilt Top Assembly

1. Assemble the Fabric B background pieces as shown, adding piece 13 last.

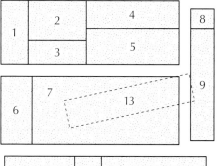

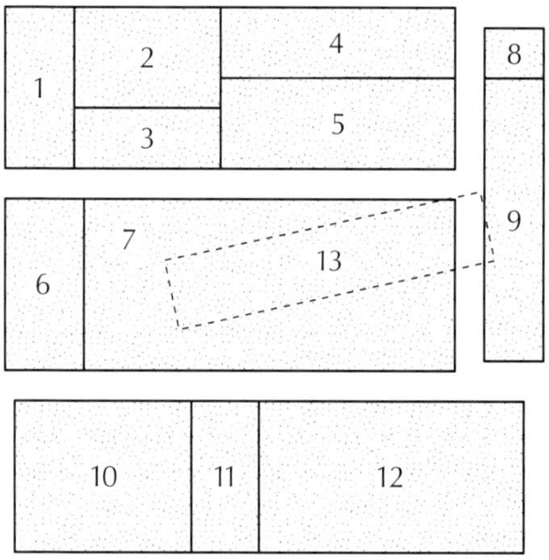

It Is Not a Woman's Desire to Be Forgotten

2. Using Fabric C and D pieces, make 1 Star block as shown. Make 4 star points, following the directions for making Flying Geese on page 21.

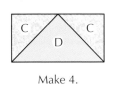

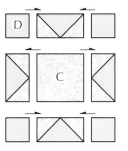

Make 4.

3. Sew 1½" x 6½" Fabric D rectangles to the sides of the star. Then sew the 1½" x 8½" rectangles to the top and bottom edges.

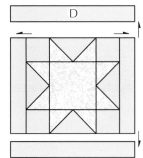

4. With right sides together, sew the Star block to the 8½" square of lightweight interfacing. Slit the interfacing and turn the block right side out. Appliqué the block on point or as shown to the lower right corner of the pieced background.

5. Using Fabric A and a ½" bias bar, make approximately 10 yards (360") of bias tubes (see page 25). Use a pencil or chalk wheel to draw the letters on the pieced background. Make each letter differently. Place the bias tubes on the drawn lines and glue them in place with the gluestick. Allow the edges to overlap.

6. Attach the letters with a running stitch, sewing along the center of each bias tube, using the dark red pearl cotton. Appliqué tight curves with regular thread (see page 25).

7. Join a Fabric E strip and a Fabric F strip to make a strip set. Make 8 strip sets. Cut a total of 54 segments, each 4½" x 4½", from the strip sets.

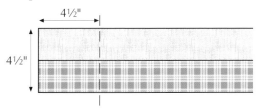

8. To make the top and bottom borders, join 13 segments end to end, flipping every other one as shown. Sew these to the top and bottom edges of the quilt top.

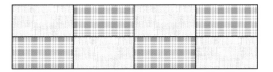

9. To make the side borders, join 14 segments end to end, flipping every other one. Sew these to the sides of the quilt top.

10. Layer the quilt top with batting and backing; baste. Quilt as desired. Bind the edges. Label your quilt.

11. Sew 3 buttons after the word "forgotten," and dot the "i's" with the remaining buttons.

TRY IT ANOTHER WAY

Appliqué photo transfers of the women in your family who inspire you, and create a lovely quilt tribute.

You can make letters with a running stitch instead of bias tubes. Use size 8 pearl cotton and a Chenille needle. Double the strand of pearl cotton to make the letters more visible.

Miracles Can Happen

By Sandy Bonsib, 1996, Issaquah, Washington, 63½" x 51½"; quilted by Becky Kraus. In the spring of 1996, we had a mother duck who sat on a nest of eggs during the day. But at night, when we put our other ducks in a pen, she often joined them, leaving her eggs uncovered for many hours. Since this was early spring and nights were cold, we assumed the eggs wouldn't hatch. Imagine our surprise when, one day after school, my daughter Kate saw a baby duck running across the mother duck's back! Kate named the firstborn Miracle, in memory of that exciting day. Miracle was soon joined by three more ducklings.

MATERIALS: 42"-WIDE FABRIC

Fabric	Single Fabric	Scrappy/First Cut	Additional Cuts
NINE PATCH BLOCKS			
A: 5 light tans	¼ yd.	20 squares, 2¼" x 2¼" (4 from each fabric)	
B: 5 medium blues	¼ yd.	25 squares, 2¼" x 2¼" (5 from each fabric)	
C: 5 colors	½ yd.	10 squares, 6¼" x 6¼" (2 from each fabric)	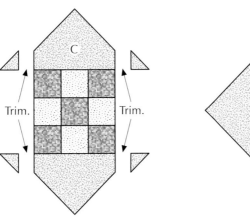
D: Background Tan 1	1¼ yds.	1 rectangle, 19" x 43", cut lengthwise	
E: Background Tan 2	⅓ yd.	1 rectangle, 10" x 37"	
F: Sky Assorted blues	⅔ yd.	52 rectangles, 2½" x 5½"	
G: Ground Assorted golds, reds & greens	1⅓ yds.	68 rectangles, 3½" x 6"	
H: Top and Right Border Assorted blues & golds	½ yd.	42 rectangles, 2½" x 3"	
Appliqué Shapes Assorted colors	1 yd.	See step 9.	
Backing	3½ yds.		
Binding (plaid)	1 yd.	6 strips, 2" x 40", cut on the bias	
Additional Supplies:	1 button for duck's eye 1½ yds. paper-backed fusible web Pearl cotton, size 8, in assorted colors Chenille needle, size 24 10" square of lightweight interfacing Assorted threads for topstitching		

QUILT TOP ASSEMBLY

1. Join 4 Fabric A and 5 Fabric B squares to make a Nine Patch block, following the directions on page 22. Sew Fabric C triangles to the sides of each Nine Patch. Press the seam allowances toward the triangles.

Make 5.

Make 5.

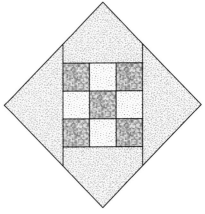

Make 5.

2. Trim the blocks to 9½" x 9½", centering the Nine Patches so the points float.

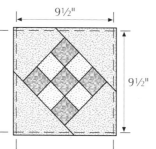

3. Join 4 Nine Patch blocks in a vertical row.
4. Join 26 Fabric F rectangles on the long edges to make a row. Make 2 rows. Join the rows.

5. Join Fabric G rectangles as follows to make the ground. I used gold rectangles in the top three rows; gold, red, and green in the fourth row; and green and red in the bottom three rows.

    Rows 1 and 2: For each row, join 8 Fabric G rectangles on the short edges. Join the rows. Trim to 43".

43"

Rows 1 and 2

    Rows 3–6: For each row, join 10 Fabric G rectangles on the short edges. Join the rows, staggering the seams. Trim to 52".

52"

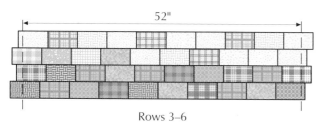

Rows 3–6

    Row 7: Join 12 Fabric G rectangles on the short edges. Trim to 61½".

6. Join 21 Fabric H rectangles on the short edges. Trim to 52½" long and 2" wide. Join to the top of the Fabric F rectangles.
7. Join another 21 Fabric H rectangles on the short edges. Trim to 51½". You will sew this to the right side of the quilt later.

8. Assemble the sections as shown.

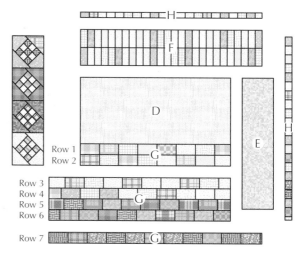

9. Prepare templates 49–59 (pages 120–26), following the "Fusible Appliqué" directions on pages 20–21. Fuse the appliqués in place, referring to the photo on page 78 for placement. Using threads that match the appliqués, machine stitch the edges of the appliqué shapes.

10. Using a running stitch and pearl cotton, stitch vertical lines on the barn (for barn siding) and cross-hatches on the silo, and outline the duck. Sew a button to the duck for an eye.
11. With right sides together, sew the remaining Nine Patch block to the 10" square of lightweight interfacing. Slit the interfacing and turn the block right side out. Appliqué the block, on point, to the lower right of the quilt top.
12. Layer the quilt top with batting and backing; baste. Quilt as desired. Bind the edges. Label your quilt.

TRY IT ANOTHER WAY

    If you have a favorite farm animal, substitute it for the duck.

Lopsided Hearts

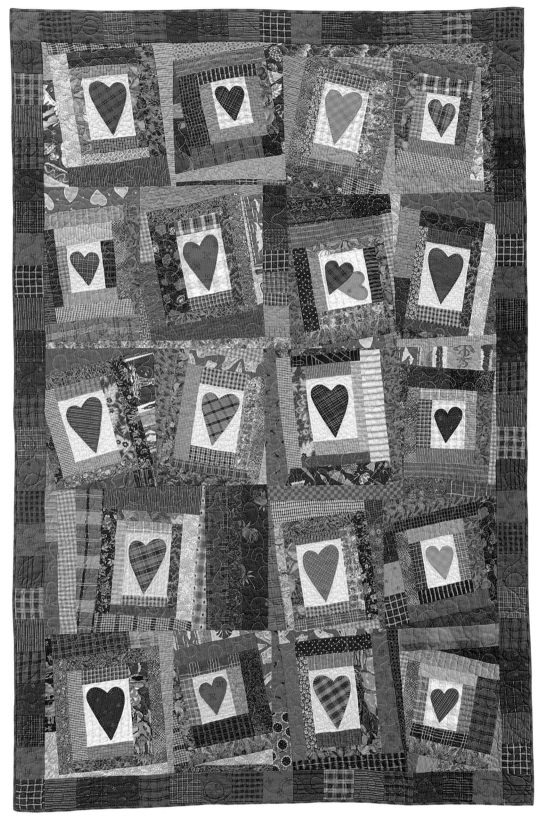

By Sandy Bonsib, 1995, Issaquah, Washington, 49½" x 72½"; quilted by Janice Nelson. This quilt combines my love of hearts with the fun of making lopsided blocks.

MATERIALS: 42"-WIDE FABRIC

Fabric	Single Fabric	Scrappy/First Cut
A: Hearts Assorted colors in medium to dark values	1 yd.	See step 1.
B: Centers Assorted light tans	¾ yd.	19 rectangles, 5½" x 6½"
C: Logs Assorted colors in medium to dark values	6 yds.*	16 strips, 1½" x 40" 16 strips, 1¾" x 40" 16 strips, 2" x 40" 24 strips, 2¼" x 40" 24 strips, 2½" x 40"
D: Pieced Borders Assorted colors in dark values	1 yd.	78 squares, 3½" x 3½"
Backing	3¼ yds. (pieced crosswise)	
Binding	⅔ yd.	260" of 2"-wide bias strips
Additional Supplies: Pearl cotton, size 8, in assorted colors		
Chenille needle, size 24		

* You probably won't need to buy 6 yards of fabric. This is a great project for using up all your leftover strips of varying widths from other projects. My narrower strips range from 1½" to 2" wide; the wider strips range from 2¼" to 2½". I used 60 to 80 different fabrics, but don't worry if you don't have that many. I suggest a minimum of 24, but more is always better. Join short strips end to end to make them longer. The scrappier your strips are, the more your quilt will look like mine. Use medium and dark strips so the center blocks will stand out. Be sure to throw some bright colors in the mediums to add life to your quilt.

QUILT TOP ASSEMBLY

1. Prepare templates 60 and 61 (page 126), following the "Fusible Appliqué" directions on pages 20–21. I made 9 small hearts and 11 large ones. Fuse the hearts to the Fabric B centers. Using pearl cotton, sew a blanket stitch around the edge of the hearts. I coordinated (not matched) the colors of pearl cotton with the heart fabrics. If you prefer, you can stitch around the hearts after finishing the blocks.

Make 19.

2. Using Fabric C strips, make 19 Courthouse Steps blocks, following the directions on page 22. Use 1½", 1¾", or 2" strips for pieces 1–4 and 2¼" or 2½" strips for pieces 5 and 6. Because the strip widths vary, the size of your blocks will vary. That's okay! If you haven't yet stitched around the edges of the hearts with pearl cotton, do that now.

These blocks look best when strips are added randomly. Put all your strips in a grocery bag. When pulling strips from your bag, don't worry if #3 doesn't look good next to #1. Exchange the strip for another only if the color or scale of the prints are the same. This applies to strips #4 and #2, #5 and #3, and all others that lie next to each other.

3. Trim the blocks as shown to get lopsided blocks. Trim one edge of a block at an angle. The first cut is the most important; the more severe the first cut, the more lopsided and smaller the block will be. After the first cut, continue around the block counterclockwise at 90° angles until all 4 sides are cut. Cut blocks that slant left as well as right, and don't cut an even number of each type.

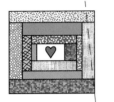

For blocks that slant right

Cut #1

90° 90° 90° 90°

Cut #2 Cut #3 Cut #4

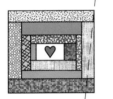

For blocks that slant left

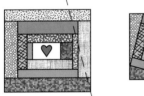

Severe initial cut

4. Arrange your trimmed blocks, 4 across and 5 down. Don't worry about blocks being different sizes. Not all your blocks need to be Lopsided Log blocks. You can add a filler to one of the rows—a leftover block from a previous project. In the quilt shown on page 81, I used leftover strips from a Rail Fence block in row 4. Play with the arrangement until you are satisfied.

5. Because the blocks are different sizes, you need to do something to them so you can sew them together. Refer to steps 2–5 of "Piecing the Quilt Top" on pages 27–28.

6. Measure the quilt top horizontally through the center. Join enough Fabric D squares to make 2 pieced borders slightly larger than the required measurement. Trim to the exact measurement and sew the pieced borders to the top and bottom of the quilt top.

7. Measure the quilt top vertically through the center, including the top and bottom borders. Join enough Fabric D squares to make 2 pieced borders slightly larger than the required measurement. Trim to the exact measurement and sew the pieced borders to the sides of the quilt top.

8. Layer the quilt top with batting and backing; baste. Quilt as desired. Bind the edges. Label your quilt.

TRY IT ANOTHER WAY

Instead of using hearts for the centers, choose a fabric with pictures or motifs. Fussy-cut the ones you want to use, adding ¼" all around for seam allowances. Remember, the centers can be different sizes. You can also transfer photos to fabric for the centers.

Stars in the Rainbow

By Sandy Bonsib, 1997, Issaquah, Washington, 66½" x 85½"; quilted by Becky Kraus. In anticipation of writing this book, I took a trip to visit folk art museums. The primitively shaped stars, designed by my quilting buddy Lynn Ahlers, were the handwork project I took on the trip. Scattered throughout the quilt, they remind me of the places I traveled as I stitched them. Lynn also helped to make the Lopsided Logs blocks.

Fabric	Single Fabric	Scrappy/First Cut
A: Stars Assorted dark reds	1 yd.	See step 1.
B: Background Assorted light tans	1 yd.	3 rectangles, 9" x 12" 6 rectangles, 9" x 11"
C: Sides Assorted dark reds	¼ yd.	3 rectangles, 1" x 12" 6 rectangles, 1" x 11"
D: Block Centers Assorted colors in medium to dark values	1 yd.	58 rectangles*, 3½" x 5½"
E: Logs Assorted colors in medium to dark values	15 yds.**	116 strips; 1½", 1¾", or 2" wide† 116 strips, 2¼" or 2½" wide†
Left and right borders Dark red	½ yd.	5 strips, 2" x 40"
Backing	5½ yds.	
Binding Dark red	⅔ yd.	9 strips, 2" x 40", cut on the straight grain

Additional Supplies: Pearl cotton, size 8, in gold, dark red, and tan
Chenille needle, size 24
Assorted red buttons

* To make a quilt that looks like mine, cut 9 purple, 16 red, 16 green, 8 blue, and 9 gold or brown centers.

** You probably won't need to buy 15 yards of fabric for the strips. Use up those extra strips you've been throwing in a box. No need to cut new strips unless you don't have enough. The narrower strips range from 1½" to 2" wide. The wider strips range from 2¼" to 2½" wide. Join short strips to make them longer. The scrappier your strips are, the more your quilt will look like mine.

†To make a quilt that looks like mine, cut 36 purple, 64 red, 64 green, 32 blue, and 36 gold or brown strips. For each color, cut half the strips in assorted smaller widths and half in assorted wider widths. For example, cut 18 purple strips that are 1½", 1¾", or 2" wide, and 18 more purple strips that are 2¼" or 2½" wide. See step 6 for additional strip sizes.

QUILT TOP ASSEMBLY

1. Using templates 62 and 63 (pages 127–28) and your favorite appliqué method, appliqué the stars to the Fabric B rectangles. Stitch small stars to small rectangles, large stars to large rectangles. Using gold pearl cotton, sew a running stitch ¼" inside the edge of each star. If you prefer, you can stitch the stars after finishing the blocks. Do not sew a running stitch around the outer edges of the stars yet.

2. Sew Fabric C rectangles to one side of each appliquéd Star block, either the right or left. Large Star blocks, including the rectangles, should measure 9½" x 12". Small Star blocks, including the rectangles, should measure 9½" x 11".

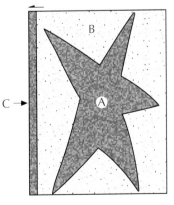

Make 9.

3. Using Fabric D rectangles and Fabric E strips, make 58 Courthouse Steps blocks, following the directions on page 22. Use 1½", 1¾", or 2" strips for pieces 1–4 and 2¼" or 2½" strips for pieces 5 and 6. Because strip widths vary, the size of your blocks will vary. That's okay! If you haven't yet stitched inside the edges of the stars with gold pearl cotton, do that now.

4. Referring to step 3 on page 83, cut your blocks askew. Trim the blocks to 9½" x 9½" including seam allowances (I used a 9½" square ruler to do this). Cut blocks that slant left as well as right, and don't cut an even number of each type.

5. Arrange Lopsided Logs blocks and Star blocks in vertical rows as shown below. Notice the placement of the small and large Star blocks. Rows 1, 3, 5, and 7 have half-blocks at the top and bottom. To make half-blocks, cut a 9½" x 9½" block to 5" x 9½". Refer to the photo on page 84 for color placement.

6. Vertical rows need to measure 85½" long. You will need to add strips to most of the rows as follows. Press all seam allowances toward the added strips.

Row One: 2 purple strips, each 1¾" x 9½". Sew one to the top of the Star block, one to the bottom.

Row Two: 1 red strip, 2" x 9½". Sew to the bottom of the Star block.

Row Three: 1 green strip, 1½" x 9½". Sew to the bottom of a Star block.

Row Four: 2 blue strips, each 1¾" x 9½". Sew one to the top of the Star block, one to the bottom.

Row Five: 1 gold or brown strip, 2" x 9½". Sew to the bottom of the Star block.

Row Six: 2 green strips, each 1¾" x 9½". Sew one to the top of the Star block, one to the bottom.

Row Seven: No additional strips are needed.

7. Join blocks in vertical rows. Join the rows.

8. Join the 2"-wide red strips end to end. From the long strips, cut 2 pieces 85½" long and sew one to each side of the quilt top. There are no borders on the top and bottom.

9. Layer the quilt top with batting and backing; baste. Quilt as desired. Using dark red pearl cotton, sew a running stitch around each star, ¼" from the edge. Some of the stitching will go beyond the background rectangles into the logs.

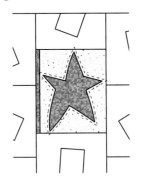

10. Sew buttons on the stars randomly—singly and overlapping in pairs. If desired, stitch small, askew stars randomly on the quilt top with tan pearl cotton. You can draw the stars freehand or reduce templates 62 and 63 with a photocopy machine.

11. Bind the edges. Label your quilt.

TRY IT ANOTHER WAY

There are many ways you could change this quilt to make it your own. Use your favorite colors instead of the ones I chose, or change the number of colors—you don't need to use five. You could also appliqué one of your favorite shapes onto the Fabric B rectangle blocks. Try your favorite animals.

Mosaic Hearts

By Sandy Bonsib, 1997, Issaquah, Washington, 36" x 33"; quilted by Becky Kraus. I created this pieced Heart block because I was tired of appliquéing hearts. The blocks are easy to cut and sew since all the pieces, including the half-square triangles, start with 1½" squares.

MATERIALS: 42"-WIDE FABRIC

Fabric	Single Fabric	Scrappy/First Cut	Additional Cuts
HEART BLOCKS			
A: Hearts 　Assorted reds, golds, greens, 　blues & purples	N/A	396 squares*, 1½" x 1½"	
B: Backgrounds 　Assorted reds, golds, greens, 　blues & purples	N/A	522 squares,** 1½" x 1½"	
C: Borders 　Red	½ yd.	2 strips, 3¼" x 27½" 2 strips, 3¼" x 30½"	
CORNER SQUARES			
D: Assorted blues	¼ yd.	4 squares, 2" x 2"	
E: Assorted purples	¼ yd.	8 squares, 2¾" x 2¾"	
Backing	1¼ yds.		
Binding	⅓ yd.	4 strips, 2" x 40", cut on the straight grain	

　* For each heart, you need 44 squares. I made 2 red, 2 blue, 2 green, and 2 gold hearts. For each color, I cut 88 squares (44 for each heart). I also cut 44 purple squares for 1 purple heart.

** For each background, you need 58 squares. I made 2 purple and 2 blue backgrounds. For each color, I cut 116 squares (58 for each background). I made 3 red backgrounds, cutting 174 red squares (58 x 3). I made 1 gold and 1 green background, cutting 58 squares for each background.

QUILT TOP ASSEMBLY

1. To make each Heart block, arrange 44 heart squares and 58 background squares, 10 squares across and 9 squares down as shown below. See the photo on the facing page for color placement. At the edges of the heart, pair 1 heart square with 1 background square, folding back the heart square to form a triangle, and pin. Step away from your block. Do you have too many lights or darks in one place? Rearrange as desired.

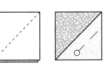

2. Sew the half-square triangle units, referring to "Method 1—Sew and Flip" on page 24.

3. Sew the squares and half-square triangle units in horizontal rows. Join the rows to complete the Heart block.

> ## TIP
>
> Before sewing these hearts together, view them through a value filter. The values may be close, and you want to be able to see the outline of the heart against the background. If necessary, make adjustments by putting lights, darks, or brights on the edge of the heart to define its shape.

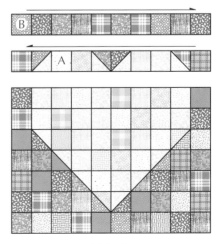

Make 9.

4. Sew the Heart blocks together in horizontal rows of 3 blocks each. Press the seams in opposite directions from row to row. Join the rows.

5. To make corner blocks, sew Fabric E triangles to the sides of Fabric D squares, following the directions for making a Square Within a Square block on page 23. Trim the corner blocks to 3¼" x 3¼", trimming equal amounts from all 4 sides.

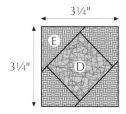

6. Add the 3¼"-wide border strips, including the corner blocks, to the quilt top, referring to "Borders" on pages 28–29.

7. Layer the quilt top with batting and backing; baste. Quilt as desired. Bind the edges. Label your quilt.

TRY IT ANOTHER WAY

These Heart blocks are really engaging. But does cutting all those 1½" squares sound like too much work? Try making only 3 Heart blocks and sewing them together in one vertical row. Add borders, and you have a wall hanging that will fit a narrow space!

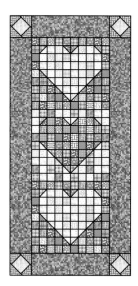

Long May It Wave

By Sandy Bonsib, 1997, Issaquah, Washington, 34½" x 48½"; quilted by Becky Kraus. Patriotic themes are a favorite among folk artists, so I couldn't resist making these flags. The wavy lines Becky quilted through some of them make the flags look as though they're really waving.

MATERIALS: 42"-WIDE FABRIC

Fabric	Single Fabric	Scrappy/First Cut	Additional Cuts
FLAGS			
A: Star Section			
Red-and-black print	¼ yd.	2 strips, 3¼" x 40"	12 rectangles, 3¼" x 4½"
B & C: Stripes			
Assorted golds	½ yd.	12 rectangles, 1¾" x 3½"	
		12 rectangles, 2½" x 7½"	
Assorted blacks	½ yd.	12 rectangles, 2" x 3½"	
		12 rectangles, 2¼" x 7½"	
D: Alternate Blocks			
Gold	¼ yd.	3 rectangles, 7" x 7½"	
E: Sashing			
Brown plaid	¾ yd.	2 strips, 2¼" x 40"	6 rectangles, 2¼" x 7½"
		3 strips, 2" x 40"	12 rectangles, 2" x 7½"
		4 strips, 2½" x 40"	20 rectangles, 2½" x 7"
F: Cornerstones			
Black	¼ yd.	2 strips, 2½" x 40"	8 rectangles, 2¼" x 2½"
			16 rectangles, 2" x 2½"
G: Borders			
Gold-and-black plaid	⅔ yd.	3 strips, 2½" x 40", for top and right borders	
		2 strips, 3½" x 40", for left border	
		1 strip, 4½" x 40", for bottom border	
H: Corner Squares			
Red plaid	¼ yd.	1 square, 2½" x 2½"	
		1 rectangle, 2½" x 3½"	
		1 rectangle, 2½" x 4½"	
		1 rectangle, 3½" x 4½"	
Backing	1⅔ yds.		
Binding	⅓ yd.	5 strips, 2" x 40", cut on the straight grain	

Additional Supplies: Black pearl cotton, size 8
Black pearl cotton, size 5
Chenille needle, size 24
Optional: 2 primitive-style metal stars

QUILT TOP ASSEMBLY

1. Arrange Fabric A, B, and C pieces as shown.
   Join the pieces to make a Flag block.

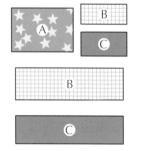
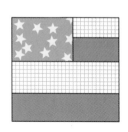

Make 12.

2. Arrange Flag blocks, alternate Fabric D rectangles, and the 2½"-wide Fabric E sashing strips as shown. Join the blocks in horizontal rows, adding a sashing strip between blocks and at the ends of each row.

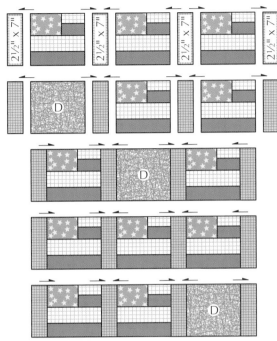

3. Make sashing rows and top and bottom inner borders as shown below.

4. Join the rows of blocks, adding 2"-wide sashing rows between the rows. Sew the 2¼"-wide sashing rows to the top and bottom edges.

5. Join the 2½"-wide border strips end to end. From the long strip, cut one 29½"-long piece and one 42½"-long piece. Join the 3½"-wide border strips end to end. From the long strip, cut one 42½"-long piece. Trim the 4½"-wide border strip to 29½".

6. Sew the side border strips to the quilt first. Sew a Fabric H corner piece to each end of the 29½" strips, matching the squares to the proper border strips as shown. Sew these to the top and bottom edges. Press the seam allowances toward the borders.

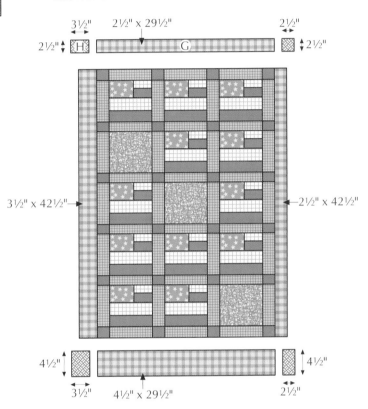

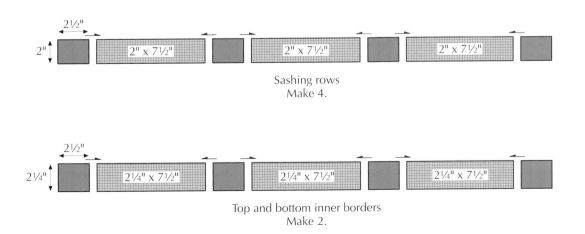

Sashing rows
Make 4.

Top and bottom inner borders
Make 2.

7. Layer the quilt top with batting and backing; baste. Using size 5 black pearl cotton, stitch words on the alternate gold blocks. Use long, overlapping stitches. Stitch ¼" inside the edges of the alternate blocks with a running stitch, using size 8 black pearl cotton.

8. Bind the edges. Label your quilt.
9. Attach metal stars, if desired.

TRY IT ANOTHER WAY

Use folk art reds, blues, and tans for a more traditional look.

I added the words after quilting because the stitches lie flatter that way. If you want to add words before quilting, you'll need to use a hoop so the fabric doesn't pucker.

Long
May It
Wave
O'Er the
Land
Of the Free
And the
Home Of
The Brave

Home Is Where You Hang Your Heart

By Sandy Bonsib, 1997, Issaquah, Washington, 46¼" x 63¾"; quilted by Becky Kraus. House blocks are a favorite with quilters, and I'm no exception. I also love simple, traditional blocks, such as the Nine Patch and Flying Geese blocks I used for the houses. Notice the unusual half-square triangle border. You can hang your heart on your favorite house.

MATERIALS: 42"-WIDE FABRIC

Fabric	Single Fabric	Scrappy/First Cut	Additional Cuts
HOUSES			
A: Assorted golds, purples & reds	½ yd.	90 squares, 2½" x 2½"	
B: Assorted golds, purples & reds	½ yd.	90 squares, 2½" x 2½"	
C: Background Assorted light tans, bubble-gum pink	1¼ yds.	40 rectangles, 1½" x 6½", for sides of houses* 40 squares, 4½" x 4½", for sides of roof*	
D: Roofs Assorted reds	¾ yd.	20 rectangles, 4½" x 8½"	
E: Sashing Turquoise	⅔ yd.	9 strips, 1¾" x 40"	15 rectangles, 1¾" x 10½" 16 rectangles, 1¾" x 8½"
F: Cornerstones Red-orange	¼ yd.	1 strip, 1¾" x 40"	12 squares, 1¾" x 1¾"
INNER BORDER			
G: Turquoise	½ yd.	3 strips, 2½" x 40" 2 strips, 1¾" x 40¼"	
OUTER BORDER			
H: Dark red	½ yd.	3 strips, 3½" x 40"	
I: Assorted tans	⅓ yd.	28 squares, 3⅜" x 3⅜" 2 squares, 3½" x 3½"	
J: Assorted reds	⅓ yd.	28 squares, 3⅜" x 3⅜" 2 squares, 3½" x 3½"	
K: Turquoise	⅓ yd.	28 squares, 3⅜" x 3⅜" 2 squares, 3½" x 3½"	
L: Corner Squares Bubble-gum pink	¼ yd.	4 rectangles, 3½" x 3⅜"	
HEART			
M: Red	Scrap	See step 15.	
Backing	3 yds.		
Binding	½ yd.	6 strips, 2" x 40", cut on the straight grain	

Additional Supplies: 4" x 6" piece of cotton batting
6" piece of jute
Tan pearl cotton, size 8
Chenille needle, size 24
1 large button

*Cut 2 squares and 2 rectangles from the same fabric for each house.

TIP

Notice that I used the same fabric for the sashing, inner border, and large triangles in the outer border. If you wish to do that, add the separate yardage amounts together so that you buy enough of one fabric. In this case, I bought 1½ yards of turquoise fabric.

HOME IS WHERE YOU HANG YOUR HEART

Quilt Top Assembly

1. Join 4 Fabric A and 5 Fabric B squares to make a Nine Patch block, following the directions on page 22. Reverse the positions of Fabrics A and B in some blocks. Make 20 blocks.

2. Sew 2 matching Fabric C rectangles to the sides of each Nine Patch block.

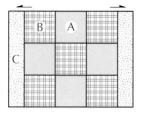

Make 20.

3. Using Fabric D rectangles and Fabric C squares that match the previously attached Fabric C rectangles, make 20 Flying Geese blocks, following the directions on page 21. These are the rooftops. Sew a rooftop to the top of each Nine Patch block.

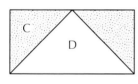

Make 20.

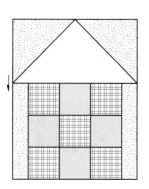

4. Arrange the House blocks, sashing strips, and cornerstones as shown at right.

5. Join the blocks in horizontal rows, adding a 10½" sashing strip between each block. Join the 8½" sashing strips and cornerstones in horizontal rows.

6. Join the rows of blocks, adding a sashing row between each one.

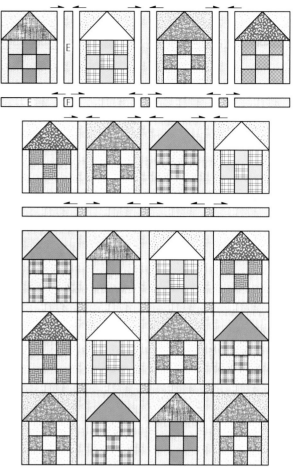

7. Join the 2½"-wide inner border strips (G) end to end. Cut 2 pieces, 55½" long. Sew these to the sides of the quilt top. Press the seam allowances toward the border. Sew the 1¾" x 40¼" strips (G) to the top and bottom edges.

8. Using pairs of 3⅜" tan (I) and red squares (J), make 28 half-square triangle units, referring to "Method 1—Sew and Flip" on page 24.

9. Draw diagonal lines on the wrong sides of the 3⅜" turquoise squares (K). Pair each square with a half-square triangle unit, right sides together, so that the drawn line runs at a diagonal to the unit's seam. Sew on the diagonal line, trim the seam allowance to ¼", and press toward the turquoise.

Make 28.

10. Join 14 units made in step 9 to make each of the top and bottom borders. Sew these to the top and bottom edges of the quilt top, positioning the light tan triangles away from the quilt top.

Make 2.

11. Join the 3½"-wide dark red border strips (H) end to end. Cut 2 pieces, each 58" long.

12. Using the 3½" tan (I) and red squares (J), make 2 half-square triangle units, referring to "Method 1—Sew and Flip" on page 24. Draw a diagonal line on the wrong side of each remaining 3½" turquoise square (K) and on the 3½" half-square triangle units. Place a turquoise square and half-square triangle unit on opposite ends of the red outer border strips as shown to make the left and right borders. Stitch on the diagonal lines. Trim the seam allowances to ¼".

13. Sew a Fabric L corner square to each end of the left and right outer border pieces. Sew the left and right border pieces to the quilt top; be sure they are positioned correctly. Press the seam allowances toward the first border.

14. Layer the quilt top with batting and backing; baste. Bind the edges. Label your quilt.

15. Using template 64 (page 126), cut 2 hearts from Fabric M and 1 heart from cotton batting. Layer the batting between the heart fabrics. Using pearl cotton, stitch a blanket stitch around the edges of the heart. Attach a loop of jute to the cleavage of the heart. Sew a button onto one House block. Hang the heart from the button.

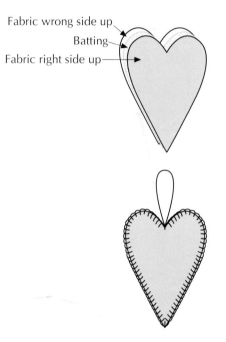

Fabric wrong side up

Batting

Fabric right side up

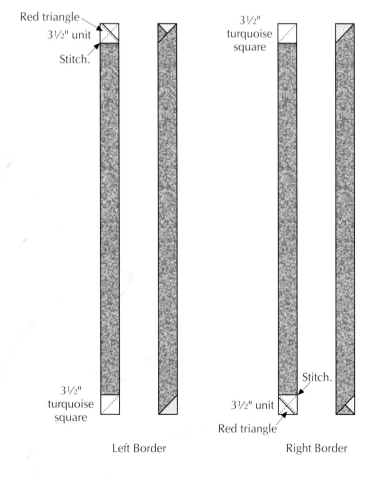

Red triangle

3½" unit

Stitch.

3½" turquoise square

3½" turquoise square

Stitch.

3½" unit

Red triangle

Left Border

Right Border

TRY IT ANOTHER WAY

Although I made my houses with Nine Patch blocks, you can use other simple, traditional blocks, for example, a Log Cabin. The blocks need to measure 6" x 6" finished (6½" x 6½" with seam allowances). See "Pieced Blocks" on pages 21–24 for ideas. You could also use a plain square for each house.

SANDY'S FAMOUS CHOCOLATE CHIP COOKIES

I have loved chocolate chip cookies as long as I can remember. Friends both young and old stop by my house on their way to and from work or school to get a cookie for the road. Five years ago, when I began teaching at In The Beginning Fabrics, I noticed that people seldom brought a snack or dinner to class, even though many of my classes were from 6 to 9 P.M. and students came right from work. People smiled more when I started bringing cookies to class, so I've never stopped!

In a large bowl, beat together:
> 2 cups (4 sticks) margarine, warmed to room temperature
> 2 cups brown sugar
> 1½ cups granulated sugar

Add and mix well:
> 2 tablespoons real vanilla extract
> 3 eggs

In a medium bowl, mix together:
> ½ teaspoon salt
> ½ teaspoon baking soda
> 6 cups all-purpose flour

Combine dry ingredients with wet ingredients, and mix well.
> (Taste the dough!)

Add 6 cups real chocolate chips (three 12-ounce bags)
> (Taste the dough again!)

Preheat the oven to 350°F. Form rounded teaspoons of dough into balls and place them on a cookie sheet, flattening them slightly. Bake for 9 to 10 minutes. If you want your cookies chewy like mine, you want the cookies only slightly done when you remove them from the oven—just starting to crack on the tops. They will finish baking on the cookie sheet. Put only one cookie sheet in the oven at a time; the cookies will cook more evenly. Let the cookies cool for at least 5 minutes on the baking sheet before removing them.

This recipe makes 120 to 140 cookies, depending on how much dough you eat! We freeze them so they stay fresh, and love them cold dipped in milk. You can warm them in the microwave for a fresh-baked taste.

BIBLIOGRAPHY

American Country: Folk Art. New York: Time-Life Books, 1990.

Amsden, Dierdre. *Colourwash Quilts: A Personal Approach to Design and Technique.* Bothell, Wash: That Patchwork Place, 1994.

Curry, David P. *An American Sampler: Folk Art from the Shelburne Museum.* Washington, D.C: National Gallery of Art, 1987.

"Folk Art." Compton's Interactive Encyclopedia. Compton's NewMedia, Inc., 1993, 1994.

"Folk Art: Striking Creations of Native Talent." *The Encyclopedia of Collectibles: Folk Art to Horse-Drawn Carriages.* New York: Time-Life Books, 1978.

Glassie, Henry. *The Spirit of Folk Art: The Girard Collection at the Museum of International Folk Art.* New York: Harry N. Abrams, Inc., in association with the Museum of New Mexico, Santa Fe, 1989.

Horton, Roberta. *The Fabric Makes the Quilt.* Lafayette, Calif.: C&T Publishing, 1995.

Hulbert, Anne. *Folk Art Quilts: Twenty Unique Designs from the American Museum in Britain.* New York: Meredith Press, 1992.

Kogan, Lee, Barbara Cate, and Gerald C. Wertkin. *Treasures of Folk Art: Museum of American Folk Art.* New York: Abbeville Press, Inc., 1994.

Lipsett, Linda Otto. *Remember Me: Women and Their Friendship Quilts.* Lincolnwood, Ill.: The Quilt Digest Press, 1997, 1985.

Oliver, Celia Y. *Fifty-five Famous Quilts from the Shelburne Museum.* New York: Dover Publications, Inc., in association with the Shelburne Museum, 1990.

Piecework Magazine, Loveland, Colo.: Interweave Press, Inc., Premier Issue, Volume 1, Number 1, March/April 1993.

Rumford, Beatrix T., and Carolyn J. Weekley. *Treasures of American Folk Art: From the Abby Aldrich Rockefeller Folk Art Center.* Boston, Mass.: Little, Brown and Co., in association with the Colonial Williamsburg Foundation, 1989.

Schaffner, Cynthia V. A. *Discovering American Folk Art.* New York: Harry N. Abrams, Inc., in association with the Museum of American Folk Art, 1991.

Walton, Stewart, and Sally Walton. *Folk Art: Style and Design.* New York: Sterling Publishing Co., 1995.

Warren, Elizabeth V., and Sharon L. Eisenstat. *Glorious American Quilts: The Quilt Collection of the Museum of American Folk Art.* New York: Penguin Studio, in association with the Museum of American Folk Art, 1996.

Wolfrom, Joen. *The Visual Dance: Creating Spectacular Quilts.* Lafayette, Calif.: C&T Publishing, 1995.

RESOURCES

PRODUCTS AND SERVICES

Sandy Bonsib
18327 SE 60th Street
Issaquah, WA 98027
Fax: (425) 644-1392
E-mail: sjbonsib@aol.com
Woodcuts on fabric

Roger Bogers
Box 552
Issaquah, WA 98027
Woodcuts

Leslie's
1404 First Avenue
Seattle, Washington 98101
(206) 467-8781
Folk art and gifts

In The Beginning Fabrics
8201 Lake City Way NE
Seattle, WA 98115
(206) 523-1121
web site: www.inthebeginningfabrics.com
*Fabrics and quilting supplies
(including Quilt Walls)*

MUSEUMS

Abby Aldrich Rockefeller Folk Art Center
307 South England Street
Williamsburg, Virginia

Museum of American Folk Art
Two Lincoln Square
New York, New York 10023-6214
(212) 595-9533

Shelburne Museum
Shelburne, Vermont
(802) 985-3346

PIECED LETTERS & NUMBERS

Cut all squares 1½" x 1½".

 Letter fabric

 Background fabric

 Half-square triangle unit (Refer to "Method 1—Sew and Flip" on page 24.)

Quarter-square triangle unit (Refer to page 26.)

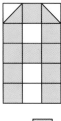  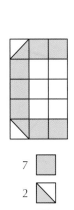 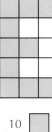 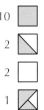

10   10   7   10   10

2   2   2   2   5

3   2   6   3

   1

 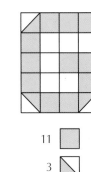 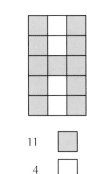 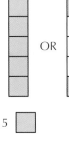 

8   11   11   5   OR   9

7   3   4   6

   6

Use this one when "I" stands alone.

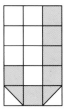 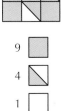 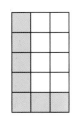 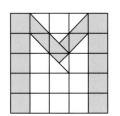 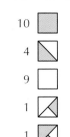

6   9   7   10   12

2   4   8   4   4

7   1   9   4

  1   1

     1

102

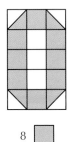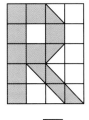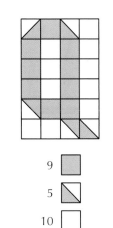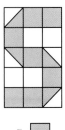

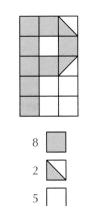

8 ⬛ 4 ◧ 3 ☐

8 ⬛ 2 ◧ 5 ☐

9 ⬛ 5 ◧ 10 ☐

8 ⬛ 6 ◧ 6 ☐

7 ⬛ 4 ◧ 4 ☐

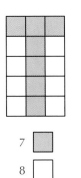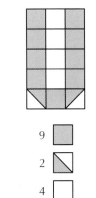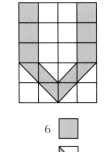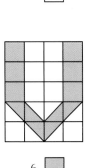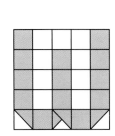

7 ⬛ 8 ☐

9 ⬛ 2 ◧ 4 ☐

6 ⬛ 6 ◧ 8 ☐

13 ⬛ 2 ◧ 9 ☐ 1 ◨

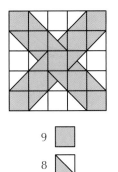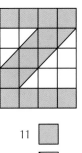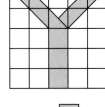

9 ⬛ 8 ◧ 4 ☐ 4 ◨

3 ⬛ 6 ◧ 15 ☐ 1 ◨

11 ⬛ 5 ◧ 4 ☐

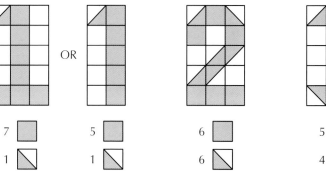

OR

7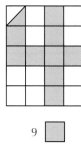
1
7

5
1
4

6
6
3

5
4
5
1

9
1
10

9
2
4

7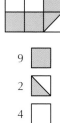
5
3

6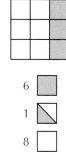
1
8

7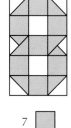
4
2
2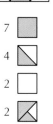

7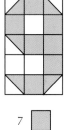
5
3

8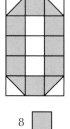
4
3

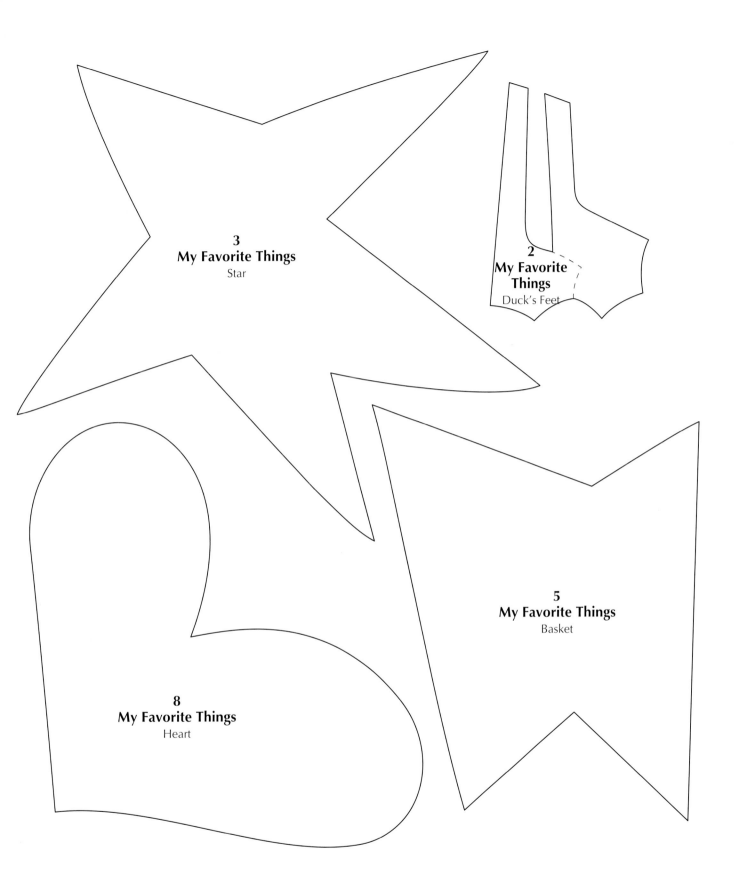

3
My Favorite Things
Star

2
My Favorite Things
Duck's Feet

5
My Favorite Things
Basket

8
My Favorite Things
Heart

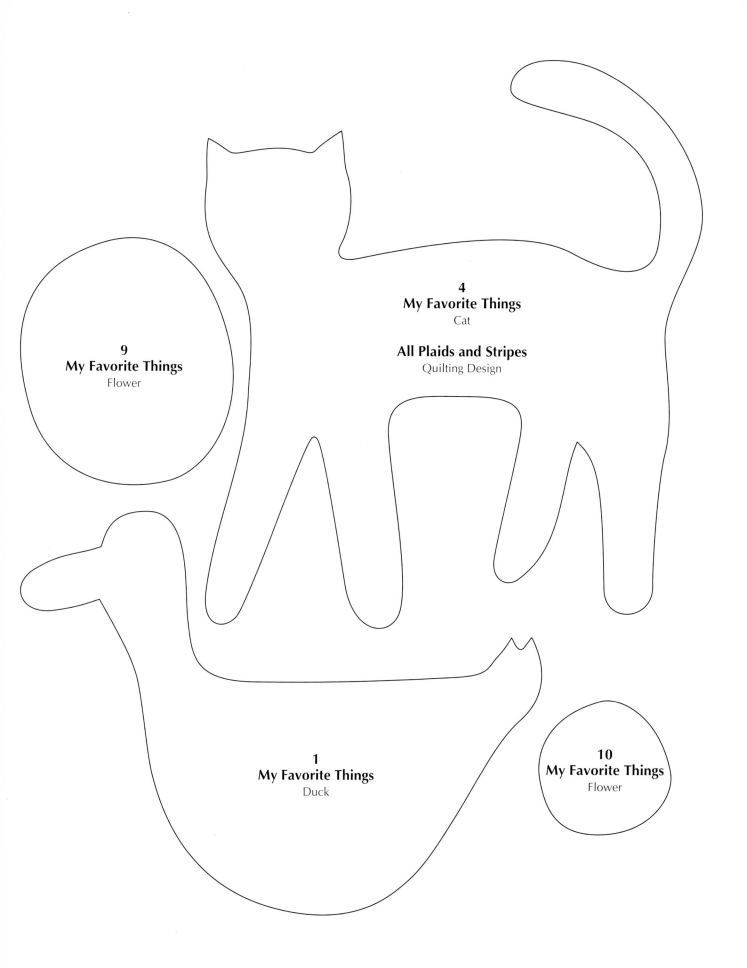

9
My Favorite Things
Flower

4
My Favorite Things
Cat

All Plaids and Stripes
Quilting Design

1
My Favorite Things
Duck

10
My Favorite Things
Flower

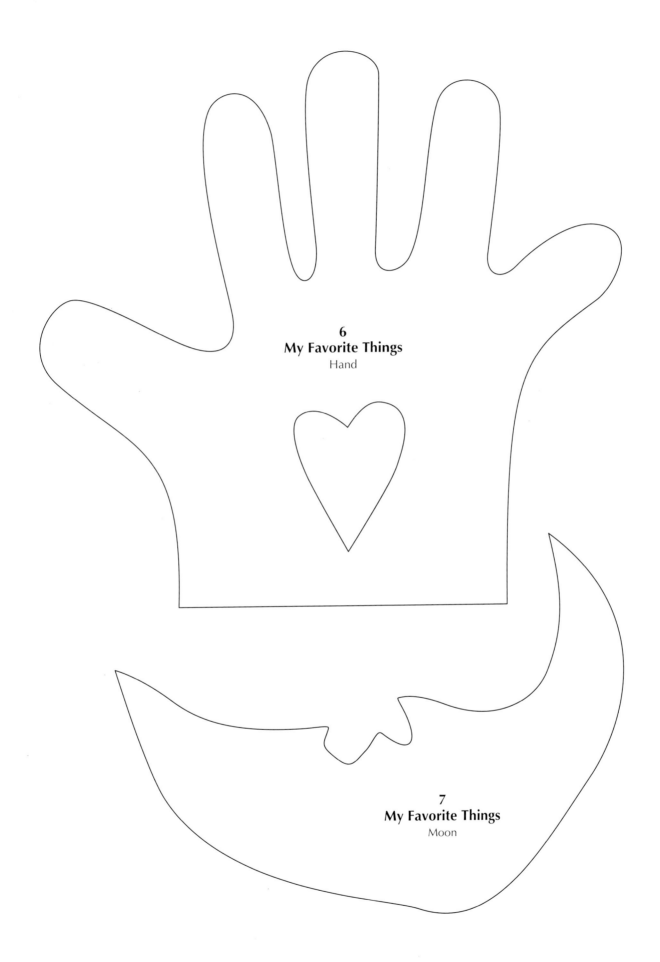

6
My Favorite Things
Hand

7
My Favorite Things
Moon

12
Coffee or Tea?
Cup

16
Coffee or Tea?
Cup

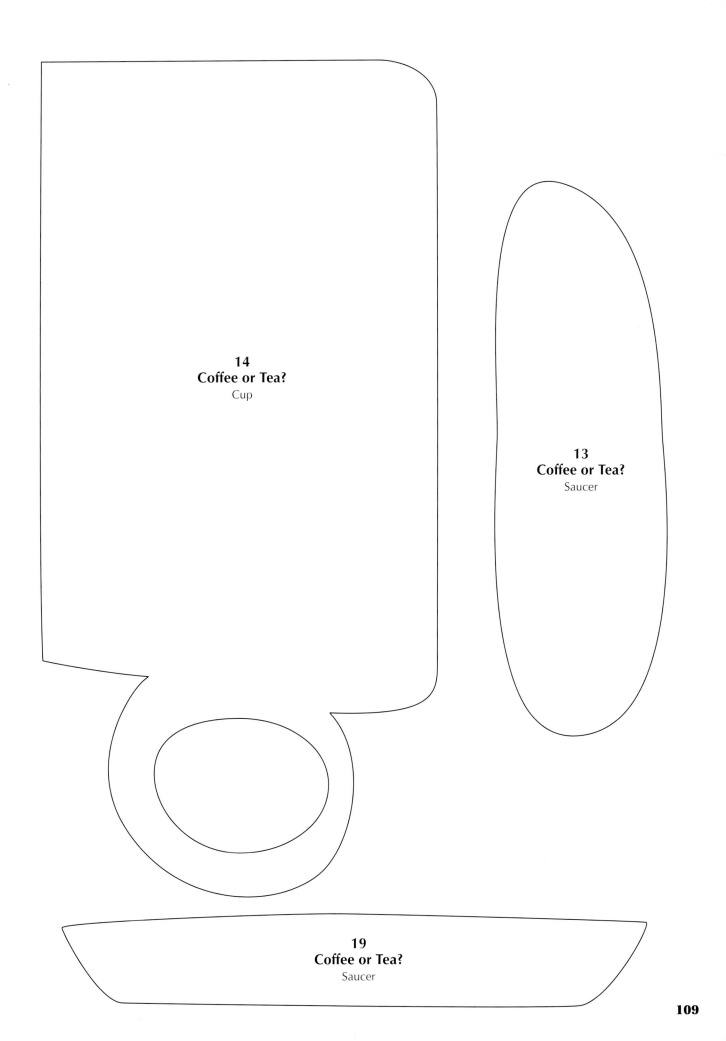

14
Coffee or Tea?
Cup

13
Coffee or Tea?
Saucer

19
Coffee or Tea?
Saucer

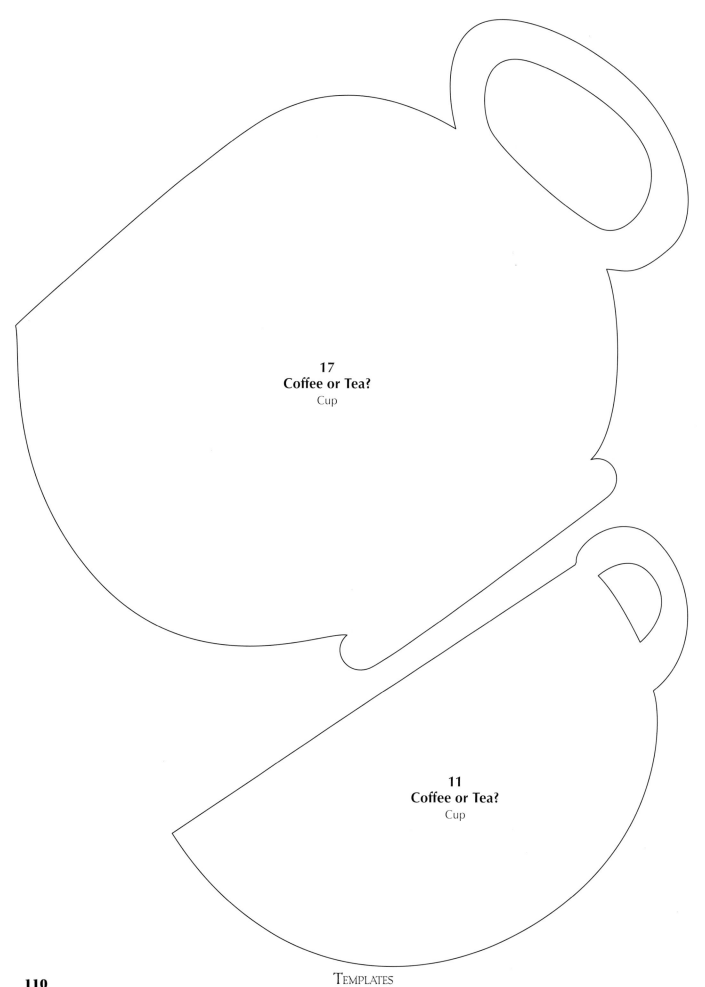

17
Coffee or Tea?
Cup

11
Coffee or Tea?
Cup

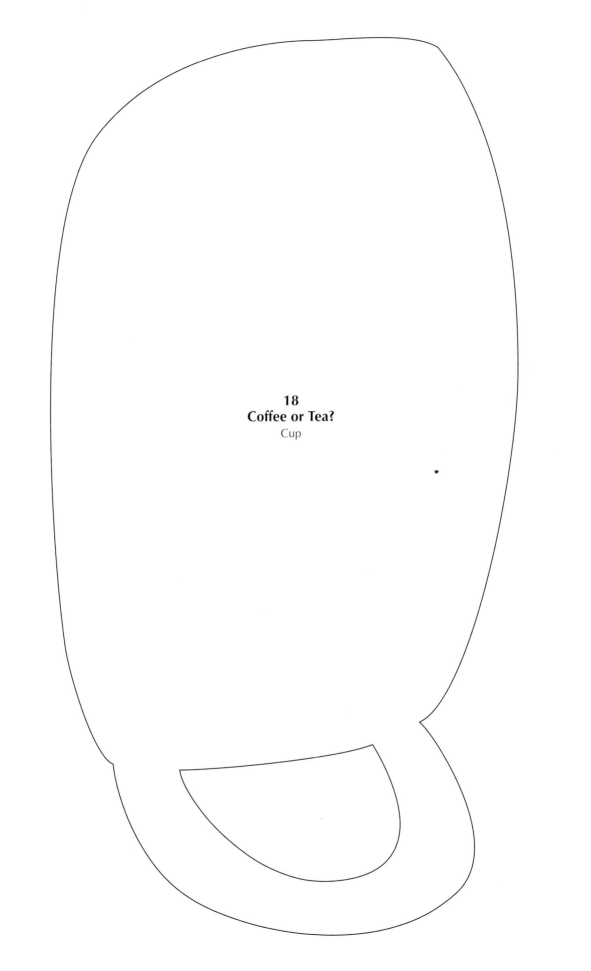

18
Coffee or Tea?
Cup

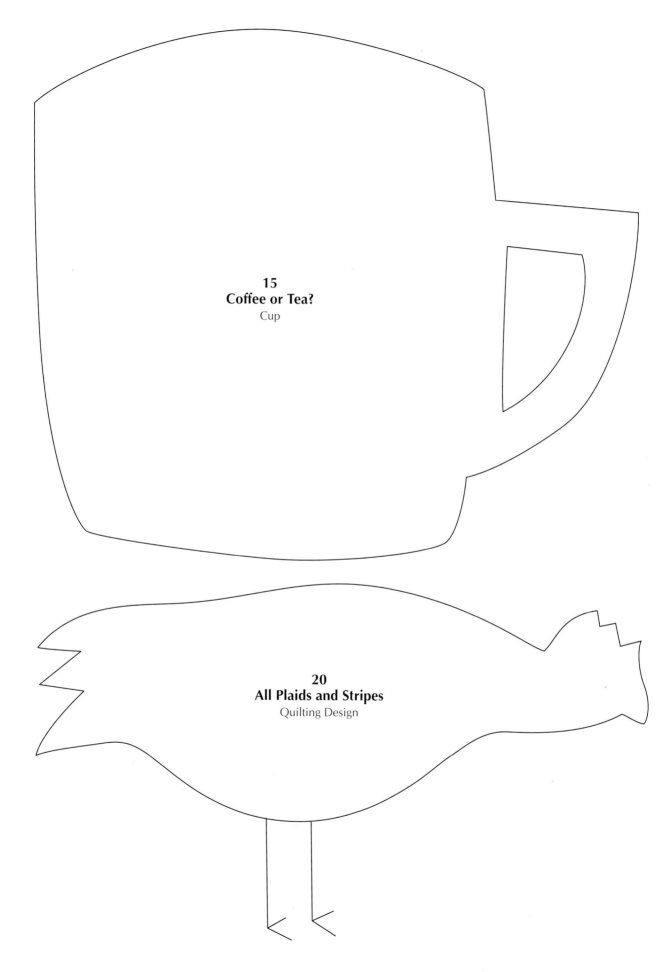

15
Coffee or Tea?
Cup

20
All Plaids and Stripes
Quilting Design

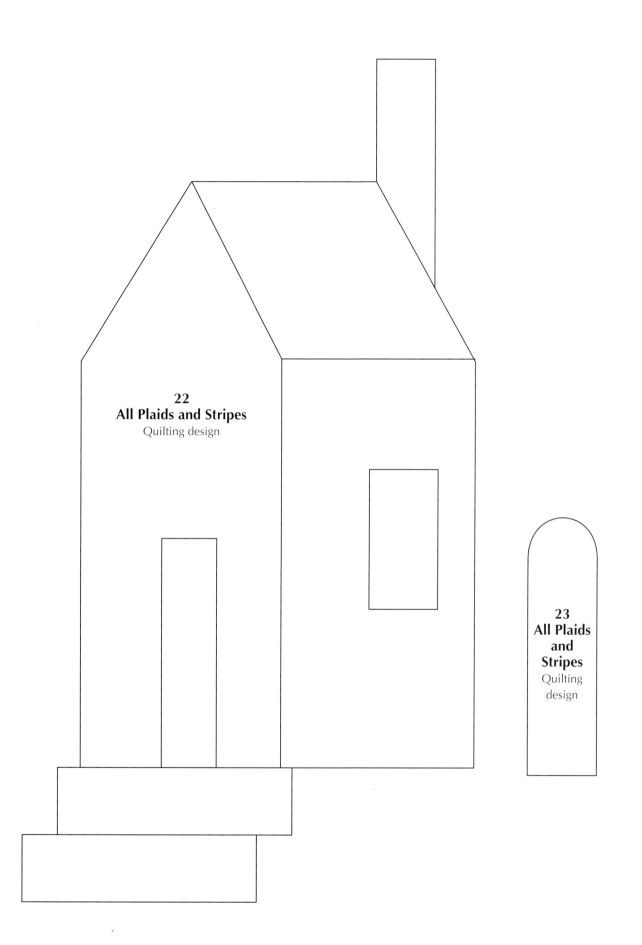

22
All Plaids and Stripes
Quilting design

23
All Plaids
and
Stripes
Quilting
design

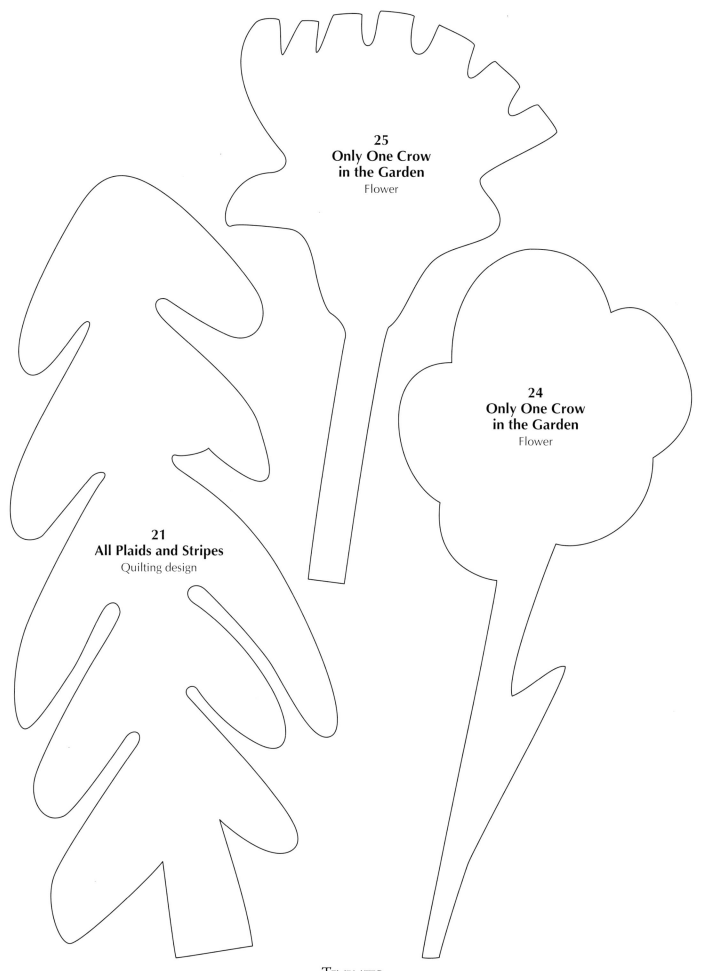

25
**Only One Crow
in the Garden**
Flower

24
**Only One Crow
in the Garden**
Flower

21
All Plaids and Stripes
Quilting design

27
Only One Crow
in the Garden
Flower

29
Only One Crow
in the Garden
Flower

26
Only One Crow
in the Garden
Flower

28
Only One Crow
in the Garden
Flower

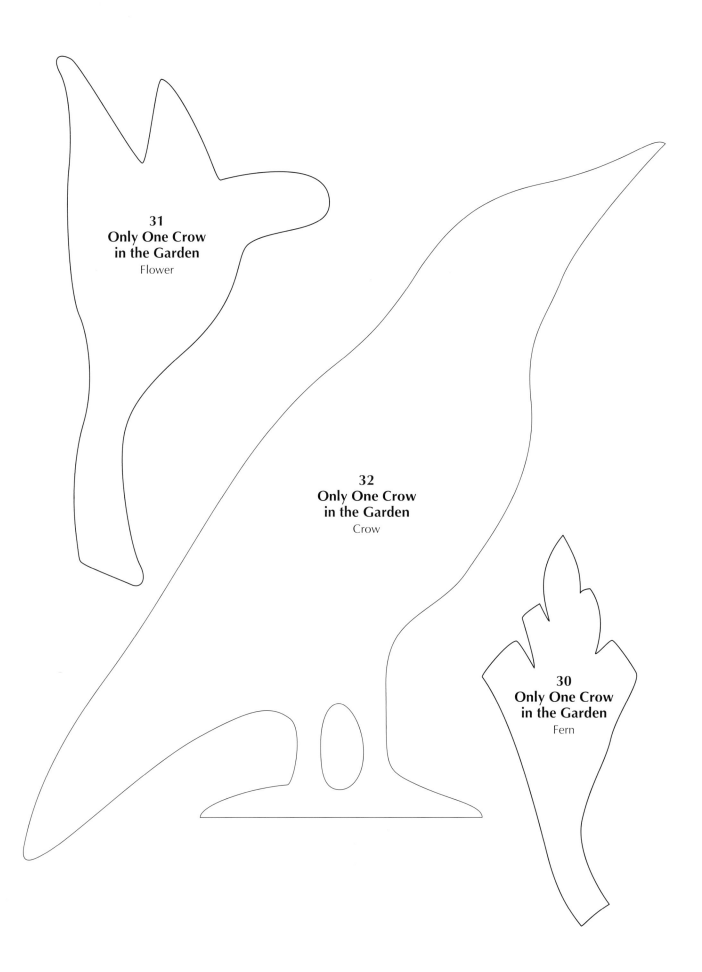

31
Only One Crow
in the Garden
Flower

32
Only One Crow
in the Garden
Crow

30
Only One Crow
in the Garden
Fern

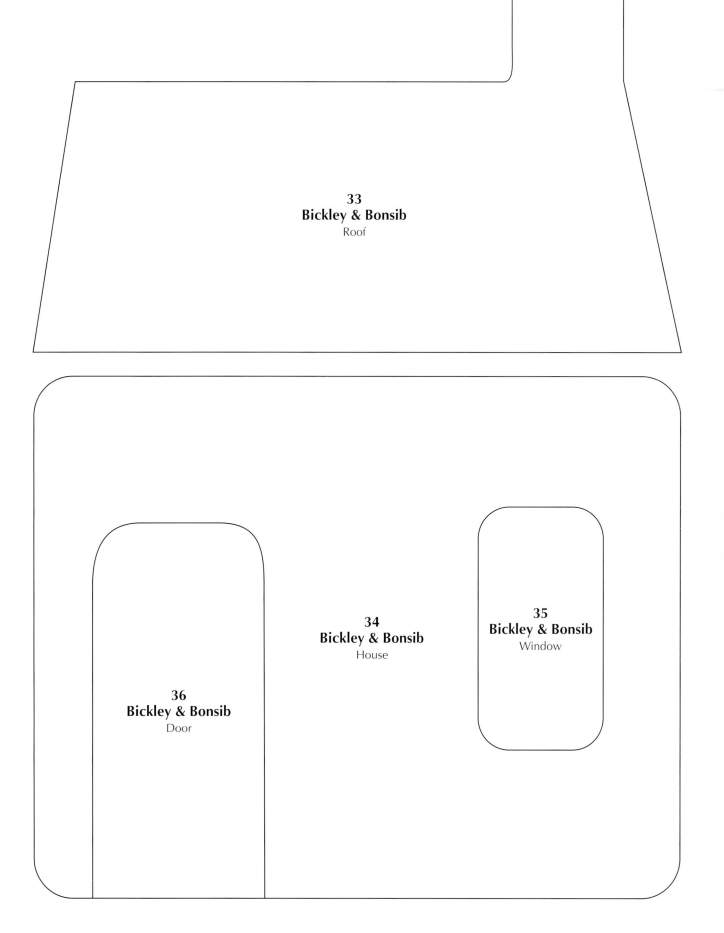

33
Bickley & Bonsib
Roof

34
Bickley & Bonsib
House

35
Bickley & Bonsib
Window

36
Bickley & Bonsib
Door

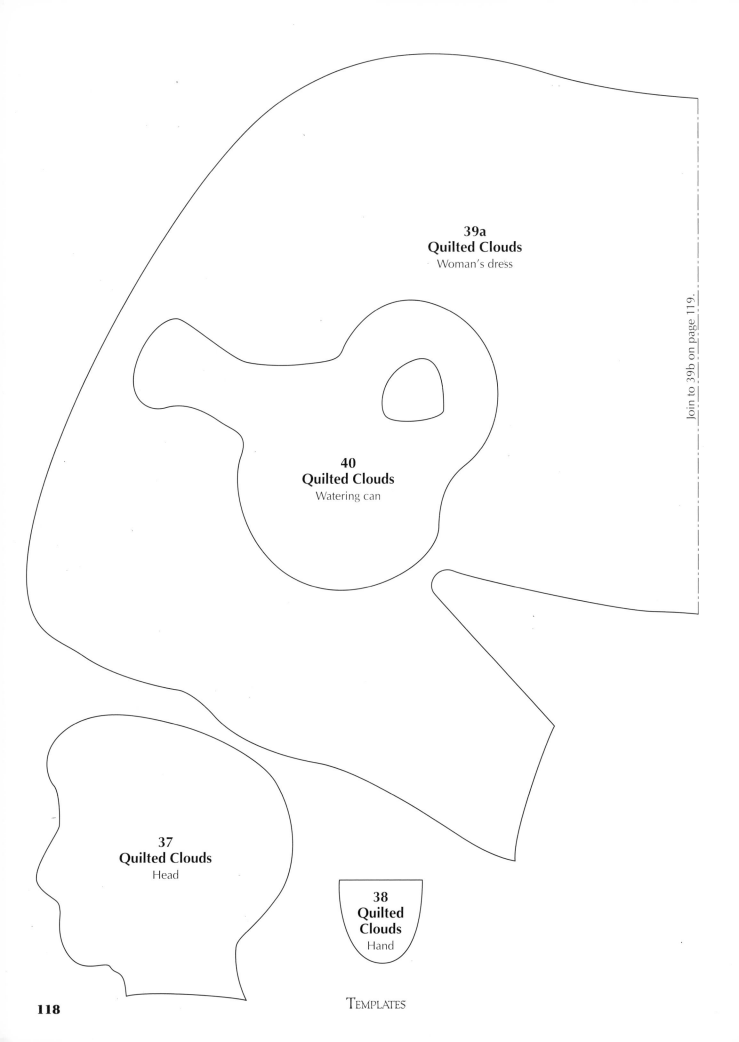

39a
Quilted Clouds
Woman's dress

40
Quilted Clouds
Watering can

37
Quilted Clouds
Head

38
Quilted Clouds
Hand

Join to 39b on page 119.

TEMPLATES

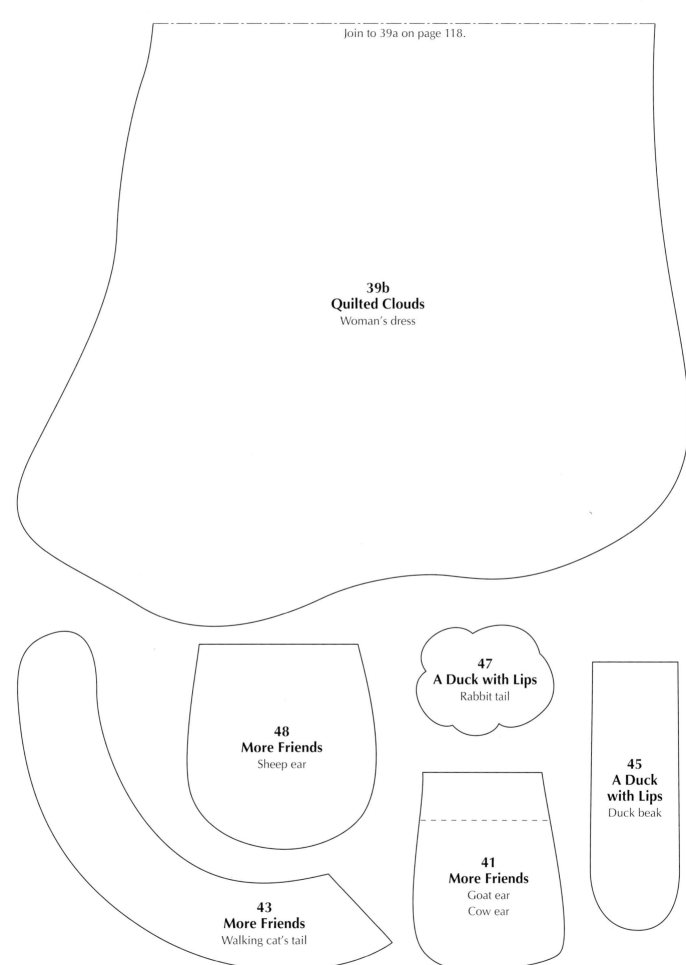

Join to 39a on page 118.

39b
Quilted Clouds

Woman's dress

48
More Friends

Sheep ear

47
A Duck with Lips

Rabbit tail

45
A Duck with Lips

Duck beak

41
More Friends

Goat ear
Cow ear

43
More Friends

Walking cat's tail

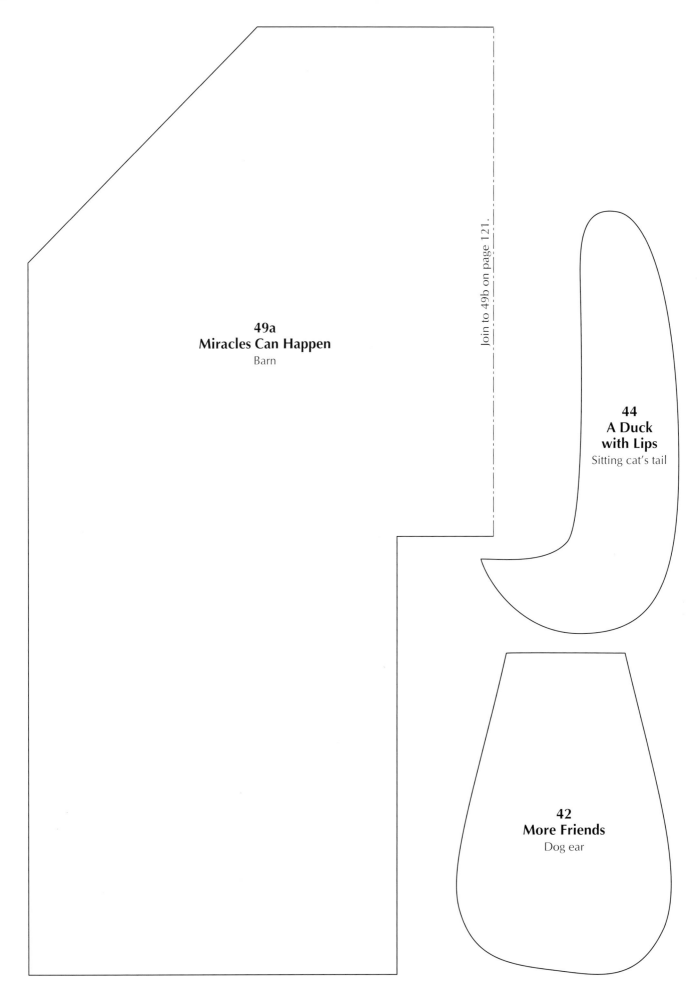

49a
Miracles Can Happen
Barn

Join to 49b on page 121.

44
**A Duck
with Lips**
Sitting cat's tail

42
More Friends
Dog ear

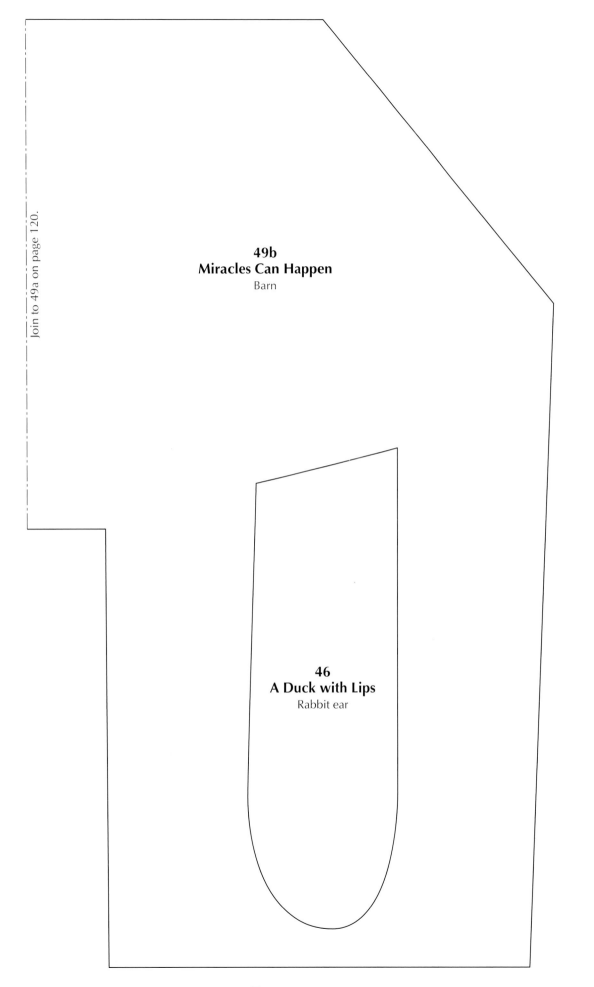

Join to 49a on page 120.

49b
Miracles Can Happen
Barn

46
A Duck with Lips
Rabbit ear

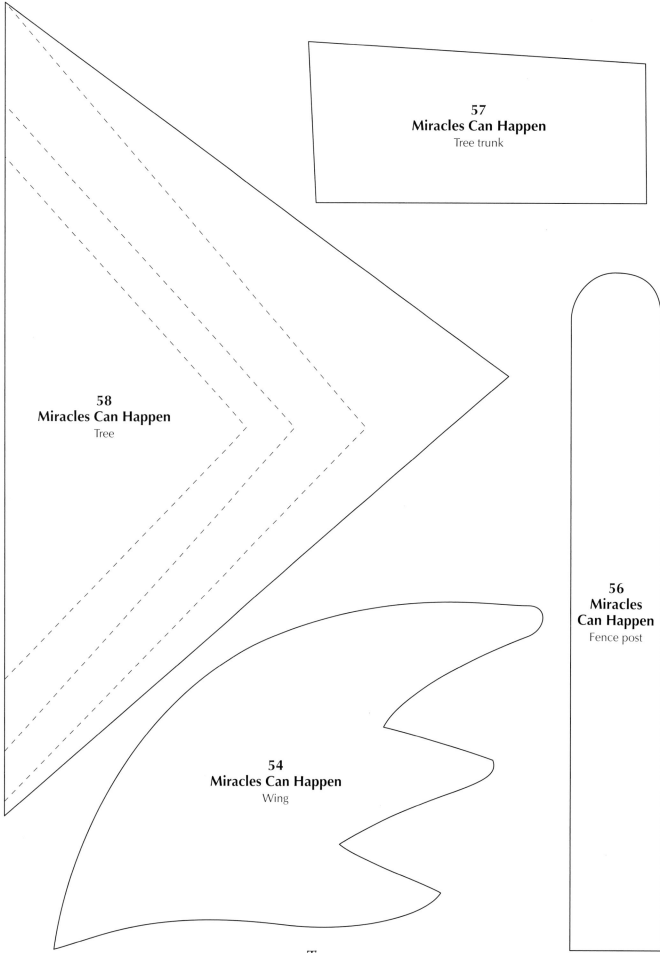

57
Miracles Can Happen
Tree trunk

58
Miracles Can Happen
Tree

56
Miracles
Can Happen
Fence post

54
Miracles Can Happen
Wing

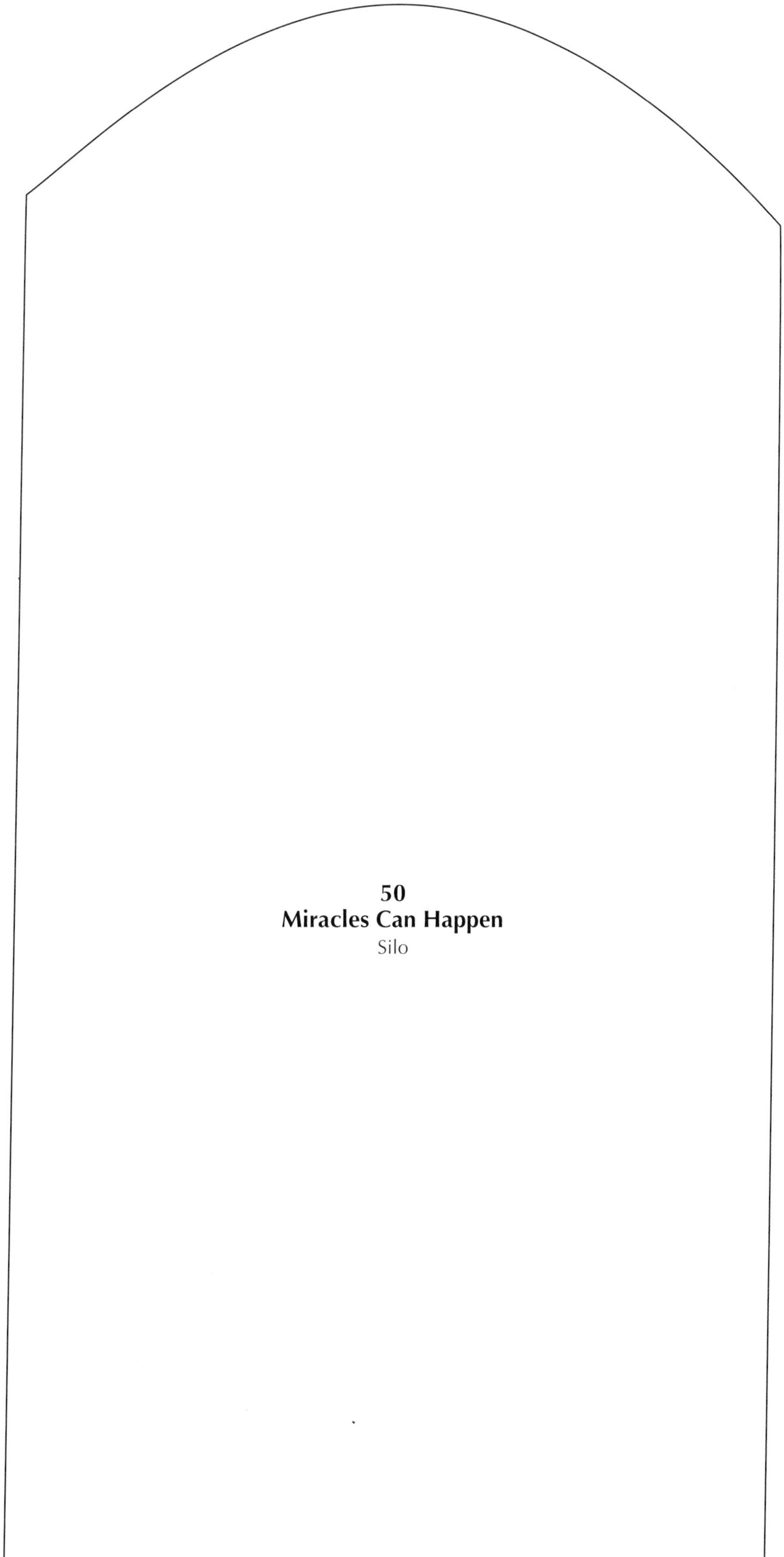

50
Miracles Can Happen
Silo

55
Miracles
Can Happen
Fence rail

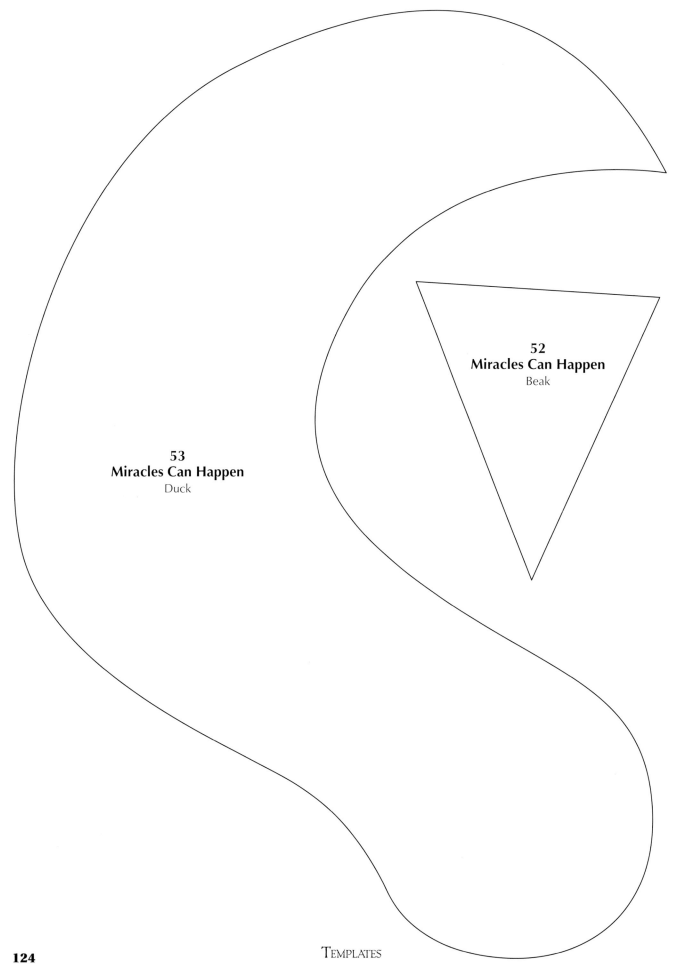

52
Miracles Can Happen
Beak

53
Miracles Can Happen
Duck

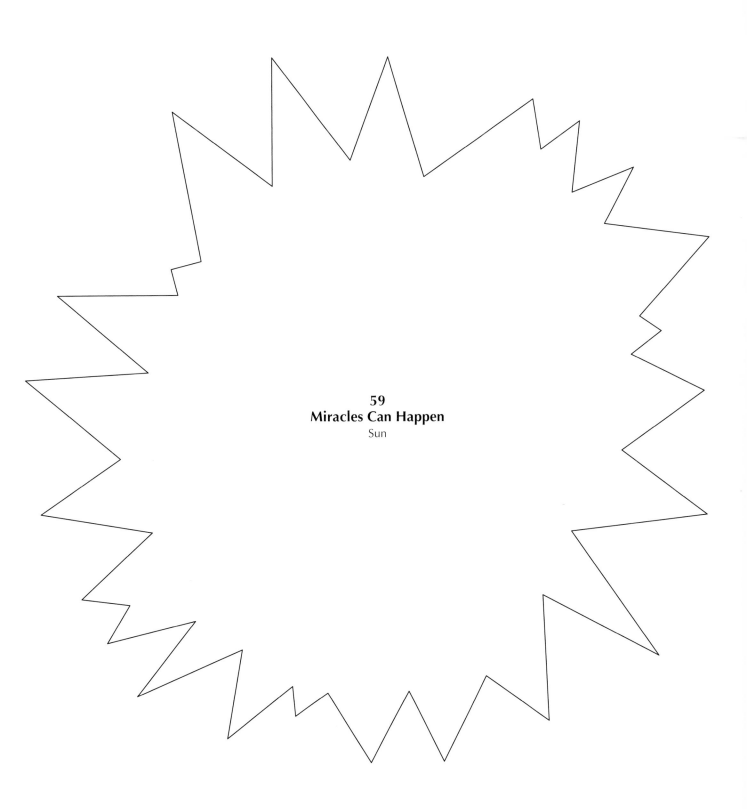

59
Miracles Can Happen
Sun

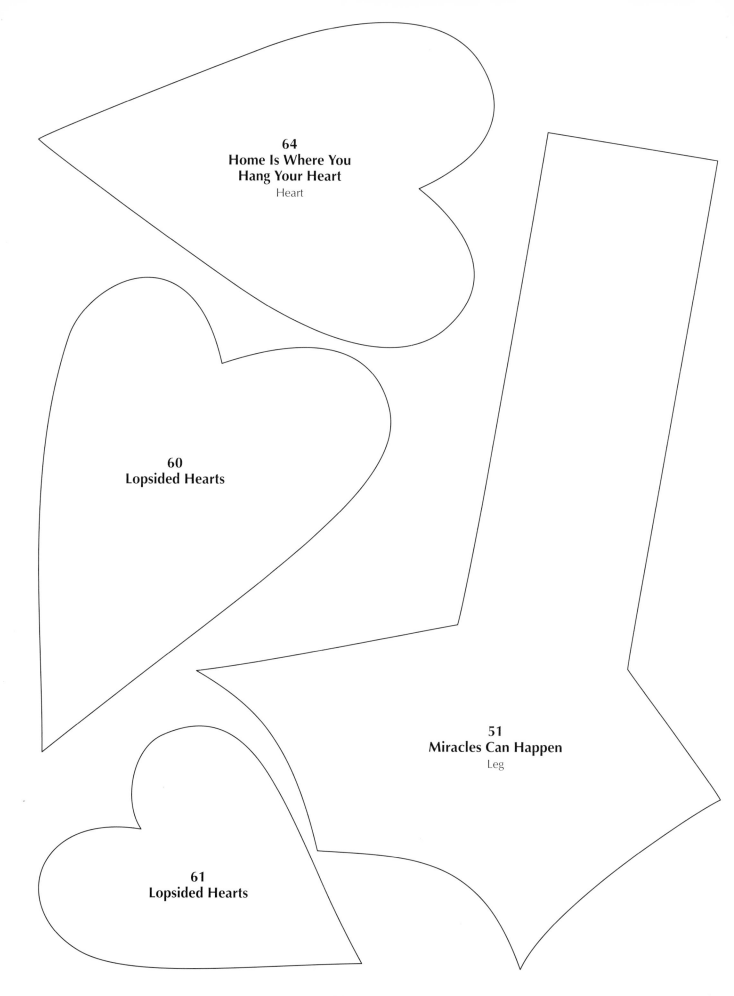

64
Home Is Where You
Hang Your Heart
Heart

60
Lopsided Hearts

51
Miracles Can Happen
Leg

61
Lopsided Hearts

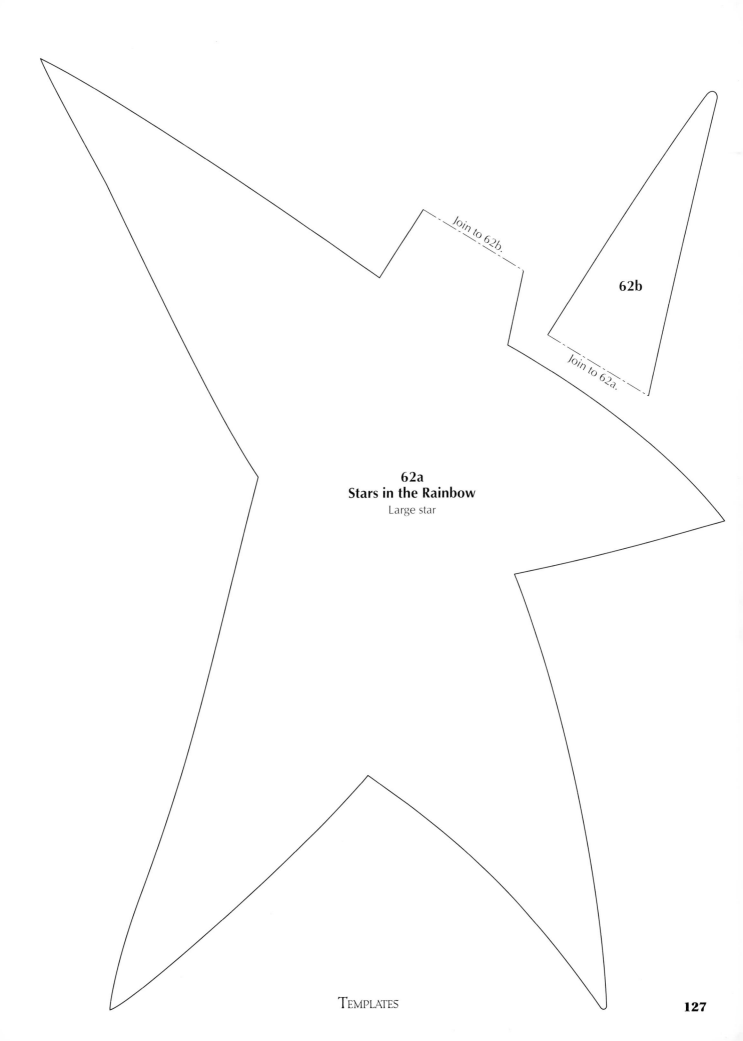

Join to 62b.

Join to 62a.

62b

**62a
Stars in the Rainbow**
Large star

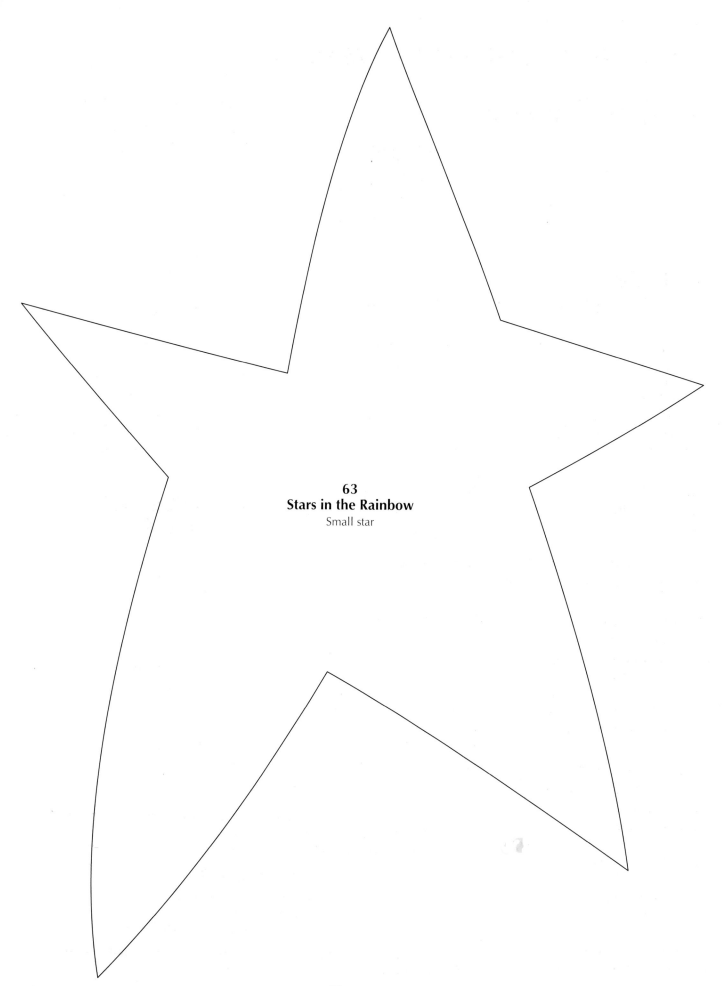

63
Stars in the Rainbow
Small star